891.723 Chekh.A Blooms
Anton Chekhov

Anton Chekhov

EDITED AND WITH AN
INTRODUCTION BY HAROLD BLOOM

CURRENTLY AVAILABLE

BLOOM'S MAJOR DRAMATISTS
- Anton Chekhov
- Henrik Ibsen
- Arthur Miller
- Eugene O'Neill
- Shakespeare's Comedies
- Shakespeare's Histories
- Shakespeare's Romances
- Shakespeare's Tragedies
- George Bernard Shaw
- Tennessee Williams

BLOOM'S MAJOR NOVELISTS
- Jane Austen
- The Brontës
- Willa Cather
- Charles Dickens
- William Faulkner
- F. Scott Fitzgerald
- Nathaniel Hawthorne
- Ernest Hemingway
- Toni Morrison
- John Steinbeck
- Mark Twain
- Alice Walker

BLOOM'S MAJOR SHORT STORY WRITERS
- William Faulkner
- F. Scott Fitzgerald
- Ernest Hemingway
- O. Henry
- James Joyce
- Herman Melville
- Flannery O'Connor
- Edgar Allan Poe
- J. D. Salinger
- John Steinbeck
- Mark Twain
- Eudora Welty

BLOOM'S MAJOR WORLD POETS
- Geoffrey Chaucer
- Emily Dickinson
- John Donne
- T. S. Eliot
- Robert Frost
- Langston Hughes
- John Milton
- Edgar Allan Poe
- Shakespeare's Poems & Sonnets
- Alfred, Lord Tennyson
- Walt Whitman
- William Wordsworth

BLOOM'S NOTES
- The Adventures of Huckleberry Finn
- Aeneid
- The Age of Innocence
- Animal Farm
- The Autobiography of Malcolm X
- The Awakening
- Beloved
- Beowulf
- Billy Budd, Benito Cereno, & Bartleby the Scrivener
- Brave New World
- The Catcher in the Rye
- Crime and Punishment
- The Crucible
- Death of a Salesman
- A Farewell to Arms
- Frankenstein
- The Grapes of Wrath
- Great Expectations
- The Great Gatsby
- Gulliver's Travels
- Hamlet
- Heart of Darkness & The Secret Sharer
- Henry IV, Part One
- I Know Why the Caged Bird Sings
- Iliad
- Inferno
- Invisible Man
- Jane Eyre
- Julius Caesar
- King Lear
- Lord of the Flies
- Macbeth
- A Midsummer Night's Dream
- Moby-Dick
- Native Son
- Nineteen Eighty-Four
- Odyssey
- Oedipus Plays
- Of Mice and Men
- The Old Man and the Sea
- Othello
- Paradise Lost
- The Portrait of a Lady
- A Portrait of the Artist as a Young Man
- Pride and Prejudice
- The Red Badge of Courage
- Romeo and Juliet
- The Scarlet Letter
- Silas Marner
- The Sound and the Fury
- The Sun Also Rises
- A Tale of Two Cities
- Tess of the D'Urbervilles
- Their Eyes Were Watching God
- To Kill a Mockingbird
- Uncle Tom's Cabin
- Wuthering Heights

Anton Chekhov

EVANSTON PUBLIC LIBRARY
1703 ORRINGTON AVENUE
EVANSTON, ILLINOIS 60201

EDITED AND WITH AN INTRODUCTION
BY HAROLD BLOOM

Plot Summary of *The Cherry Orchard*	79
List of Characters in *The Cherry Orchard*	84
Critical Views on *The Cherry Orchard*	
Maxim Gorky on Chekhov's Tragic Humor	86
Francis Fergusson on the Suffering of Change in *The Cherry Orchard*	88
Ilya Ehrenburg on the Shadings of Character in Chekhov's Works	90
Maurice Valency on the World of *The Cherry Orchard*	93
John Tulloch on *The Cherry Orchard* in a Political Scheme	95
Donald Rayfield on the Ideas Behind *The Cherry Orchard*	97
Works by Anton Chekhov	99
Works about Anton Chekhov	100
Index of Themes and Ideas	103

User's Guide

This volume is designed to present biographical, critical, and bibliographical information on the playwright's best-known or most important works. Following Harold Bloom's editor's note and introduction are a detailed biography of the author, discussing major life events and important literary accomplishments. A plot summary of each play follows, tracing significant themes, patterns, and motifs in the work.

A selection of critical extracts, derived from previously published material from leading critics, analyzes aspects of each play. The extracts consist of statements from the author, if available, early reviews of the work, and later evaluations up to the present. A bibliography of the author's writings (including a complete list of all works written, cowritten, edited, and translated), a list of additional books and articles on the author and his or her work, and an index of themes and ideas in the author's writings conclude the volume.

~

Harold Bloom is Sterling Professor of the Humanities at Yale University and Henry W. and Albert A. Berg Professor of English at the New York University Graduate School. He is the author of over 20 books and the editor of more than 30 anthologies of literary criticism.

Professor Bloom's works include *Shelley's Mythmaking* (1959), *The Visionary Company* (1961), *Blake's Apocalypse* (1963), *Yeats* (1970), *A Map of Misreading* (1975), *Kabbalah and Criticism* (1975), and *Agon: Toward a Theory of Revisionism* (1982). *The Anxiety of Influence* (1973) sets forth Professor Bloom's provocative theory of the literary relationships between the great writers and their predecessors. His most recent books include *The American Religion* (1992), *The Western Canon* (1994), *Omens of Millennium: The Gnosis of Angels, Dreams, and Resurrection* (1996), and *Shakespeare: The Invention of the Human* (1998), a finalist for the 1998 National Book Award.

Professor Bloom earned his Ph.D. from Yale University in 1955 and has served on the Yale faculty since then. He is a 1985 MacArthur Foundation Award recipient, served as the Charles Eliot Norton Professor of Poetry at Harvard University in 1987–88, and has received honorary degrees from the universities of Rome and Bologna. In 1999, Professor Bloom received the prestigious American Academy of Arts and Letters Gold Medal for Criticism.

Currently, Harold Bloom is the editor of numerous Chelsea House volumes of literary criticism, including the series BLOOM'S NOTES, BLOOM'S MAJOR SHORT STORY WRITERS, BLOOM'S MAJOR POETS, MAJOR LITERARY CHARACTERS, MODERN CRITICAL VIEWS, MODERN CRITICAL INTERPRETATIONS, and WOMEN WRITERS OF ENGLISH AND THEIR WORKS.

Editor's Note

My Introduction ponders the subtle relation of Chekhov's four major plays to Shakespeare.

Of the two dozen critical extracts, all of them highly useful, I particularly commend those by Richard Gilman, Eric Bentley, Maxim Gorky, and Francis Fergusson. The great problem of Chekhov criticism is how to say just enough without falling into redundancy; for this we must follow the example of Chekhov's own subtle art as a dramatist.

Introduction
HAROLD BLOOM

Of his friend Anton Chekhov, Russian author Maxim Gorky once commented that in his presence "everyone felt an unconscious desire to be simpler, more truthful, more himself." That seems to me the desire also of the viewer and reader of Chekhov's plays. *The Seagull*, one of *Hamlet*'s many children, features in Trigorin Chekhov's own outrageous self-parody, which is also a parody of the Prince of Denmark. But so is Konstantin, and so perhaps is the high-minded young actress, Nina.

We return to *Hamlet* in the title character of *Uncle Vanya*, who plays at suicide, but is not resolute enough for it, as Eric Bentley remarks. The lid stays on in Chekhov, Bentley also says—of all playwrights, Chekhov is the least Promethean. Shakespeare, unlike Bentley's Chekhov, is not much interested in what might have been; so much goes on in *Hamlet* that we have trouble keeping it straight. The unlived life could hardly be a concern of the creator of Falstaff and Cleopatra; it is the unique obsession of Chekhov, or rather, of his major characters.

Hamlet is not much interested in his play's other characters; he does not care enough about Claudius to kill him until it is already too late, but then one doubts that Hamlet cares that much about Gertrude, Ophelia, Horatio, or even the dead father, despite all Hamlet's protestations. Chekhov shrewdly saw this; his major characters emulate Hamlet by indulging in long monologues, and by a gorgeous solipsism, in which all other personages become surrogates for the audience. Perhaps Hamlet is the more overt model in *The Seagull* and *Uncle Vanya*, but his presence hovers still in the far subtler *The Three Sisters* and *The Cherry Orchard*. Is Hamlet tragic or comic? We never can answer, and the Prince's amalgam of the two antithetical modes sets the paradigm for Chekhov.

The Three Sisters depends upon the complex ways in which Olga, Masha, and Irina, together with their brother Andrey, constitute a fourfold parody of Prince Hamlet. Masha inherits Hamlet's function of intolerable truth-telling, while Irina reincarnates the Prince's inability to return the love that he provokes. Olga, like Hamlet, incarnates the good, without knowing it and therefore without being able to defend it. Andrey Prozorov, though not created on the Shakespearean scale of his sisters, is nevertheless an artist, like the Hamlet who revises *The Murder of Gonzago* into *The Mousetrap*. Together, the three sisters and their brother provoke our love, because they do not transcend us, as Hamlet does. The sisters proclaim that they do not know enough, whereas Hamlet knows the truth, and perishes of it. We are grateful that Masha, Irina, and Olga survive, and so we are glad that they know less than Hamlet did.

The Cherry Orchard, an equally rich drama, is something of a Shakespearean farce, but then so are certain aspects of *Hamlet*. The beautiful and tragic Lyubov is beyond farce, like Shakespeare's Cleopatra, but the wonderful Lopakhin is even more Shakespearean, forceful yet nostalgic, a wise fool, hard but benign, almost a Falstaff whose Prince Hal is the unattainable Lyubov. Like Falstaff, Lopakhin tells the truth, which in Chekhov as in Shakespeare is always the triumph of change, even when there is no will to change. ❧

Biography of Anton Chekhov

Anton Pavlovich Chekhov was born on January 17, 1860, in Taganrog, a provincial Russian town on the Sea of Azov. He was the third son of a merchant, and the grandson of serfs. Both of his grandfathers had been born into serfdom and both of them managed to buy themselves and their families out of slavery. Two generations later, Anton was a famous writer and social activist.

Chekhov's father, Pavel, was a cruel, tyrannical man who sermonized endlessly. Though his sons would later have painful memories of the brutal upbringing their father gave them, they also found humor in their father's incessant grandstanding. He kept a shop in Taganrog and employed his three eldest sons, Aleksandr, Kolia (Nikolai), and Anton, from very early ages. In spite of the Chekhov children's violent, relentlessly difficult childhoods, they were a close, ebullient family and would remain so throughout their lives.

In 1876, Anton's father, Pavel, left Taganrog under cover of night to escape his creditors. He was deeply in debt and would not be free of financial obligation again until Anton became a literary success. Pavel moved in with his two eldest sons in Moscow, where they were attending university. He lived off the money they were able to scrape together, even though the sons themselves were impoverished to the point of near-starvation. Back in Taganrog, he left fifteen-year-old Anton to keep up a household that included his mother and his three younger siblings. This was the beginning of a pattern of dependency on Anton that would not change again. By the time he was in his mid-twenties, Anton was supporting everyone in his family. His first play, written in 1877, is entitled *Fatherlessness*.

In the fall of 1879, Chekhov entered medical school in Moscow. In March 1880 he published his first short story and in November of 1882 he began to publish weekly in a magazine called *Fragments*, becoming a regular contributor. This was not merely literary drive, but his chief means of providing for his dependents. In 1884 he graduated from Moscow University Medical School, and in June of that year his first collection of short stories was published.

His literary reputation grew, and he acquired a life-long publisher and friend, Aleksey Suvorin. In 1887 he won the Pushkin Prize for literature.

These successes were dimmed by the constant presence of illness, however. Chekhov had tuberculosis from an early age, and in 1884 at the age of twenty-four, he experienced his first serious hemorrhage. From this point, his health would gradually deteriorate, with a number of extended remissions, until his death at the age of forty-four.

How early Chekhov knew his fate is not known, but having been a doctor who saw a vast number of friends and relatives suffer and die from TB, including his brother Kolia (Nikolai), he must have known he would not live long. Kolia's death in 1889, was deeply disturbing for Chekhov. Although Kolia had been a talented painter, he had sunk into a bottomless depression (generally perceived as laziness) years earlier and had never recovered. This depressive tendency would manifest itself in all the Chekhov siblings from time to time, though Anton would surmount it with endless work and social activity.

In 1890, Chekhov left Moscow to travel across perilous Siberia and visit the grim penal colony at Sakhalin Island. Acting as doctor rather than writer, he did a sociological study of the people there and came back to write a nonfiction book about his experiences. On his way back he traveled through Hong Kong, Singapore, Ceylon, and Port Said.

In 1892 he fulfilled a life-long dream of purchasing a country estate in Melikhovo. He became the owner of over five hundred acres, two ponds, a house, an orchard, horses, cows, and dogs. When he saw the amount of work necessary to maintain the estate, he was for a time aghast at his decision to buy it, but he eventually came to love it.

He helped fight the cholera epidemic in the region, and he became a local benefactor, building schools and clinics for the peasants. Here at Melikhovo he wrote his first major play, *The Seagull*. In October of 1895, the first performance of *The Seagull* took place in the Aleksandrinsky Theater in Petersburg. The reception was mediocre, and the play bordered on failure. Chekhov was despondant. In 1897 he was hospitalized for tuberculosis and in 1899 he was forced to move to Yalta to improve his health.

December 17, 1898, was the inauguration of the Moscow Art Theater, founded by the great theater theorist and teacher Constantin Stanislavsky, and *The Seagull* was produced in its first season—with great success this time. In the following year, the Moscow Art Theater produced *Uncle Vanya*, and then in 1901 they produced *The Three Sisters*. In May of 1901, Chekhov married a prominent actress of the Moscow Art Theater, Olga Knipper.

In February of 1902, Chekhov received a telegram that his friend and fellow-writer Maxim Gorky had been elected an honorary member to the prestigious Academy of Sciences, of which he himself was a member. Two weeks later, the literary world learned that Gorky's election had been rescinded because of new information about his prison record—Gorky was a budding Marxist and had been politically active in a highly censored society. When Chekhov learned of this, he ended his own membership. This renunciation was a major event in Russian political and academic circles.

Chekhov's last play, *The Cherry Orchard*, premiered on January 17, 1904, at the Moscow Art Theater, in honor of his 44th birthday and in celebration of his 25th anniversary of literary work. Soon after he traveled to Germany in a vain attempt to improve his health. On July 2nd he died. His body was returned to Russia on a train car meant for the transportation of oysters—an irony Chekhov would undoubtedly have appreciated. ❧

Plot Summary of
The Seagull

It is late nineteenth-century Russian and a motley gathering of people are visiting the country estate of Pyotr Sorin, each of them amorously yearning for someone who does not reciprocate their feelings. As the play opens, Medvedenko, a teacher, is pursuing the young Masha, daughter of the estate steward, as they walk around the grounds. They pass a shoddily built stage on which an amateur play will appear that evening. The opening line is Medvedenko's; he asks Masha why she always wears black. Her famous reply is, "I am in mourning for my life. I'm unhappy."

The Seagull was meant to be a comedy, a fact that is often overlooked. The downward spiral of the characters' lives can be deceiving, and the play is often staged as a melodrama. The action of this play, as with all Checkhov's plays, does not necessarily move forward but lolls in little pools of interaction between people who lament and pontificate at length, but actually do very little while they are on stage. In his four major plays, the action generally happens off-stage or between acts. The technique of burying the plot like this is distinctly Chekhovian. *The Seagull*'s comedy comes from parody. Chekhov subtly satirizes the problems of his characters, and if we look closely at Checkhov's life at the time he was writing the play, we can see that he was privately satirizing his circle of intimates—a very overwrought and histrionic group of people whose lives in turn-of-the-century Russia were little short of high drama.

The Seagull was the first play that the Moscow Art Theater, co-founded by Stanislavsky and Nemirovich-Danchenko, would produce. To this day, the Moscow Art Theater displays an image of a seagull on its stage curtain. This famous theater's main innovation was the termination of the star system and the introduction of ensemble acting. No more would a play serve as a vehicle for one or two stars. Ensemble acting would revolutionize theater, and *The Seagull*, written several years before the inception of the Moscow Art Theater, would foretell Stanislavky's new method of realistic acting. *The Seagull* is without a starring character. It is a group portrait. In fact, in *The Seagull* Chekhov parodies the star system by drawing the character of Arkadina, the ego-maniacal, vacuous actress.

The Seagull's central question is about art. The four major characters are all artists and their principal preoccupations are about how to approach their art. In the **first act**, the people on Sorin's estate gather to watch the little one-character play, written by Treplyov, as it is performed by the lake with the moon rising in the background. Treplyov is Sorin's nephew and the only son of the famous actress, Arkadina, who is in the audience. He has written a highly unusual little play, declaring that he is searching for "new forms." His play is abstract in the extreme, and it is quickly a miserable failure. Treplyov calls off the play only minutes after it has begun. The one character declares, " Cold, cold, cold. Empty, empty, empty. Frightful, frightful, frightful."

While Treplyov's dramatic venture cannot be called anything but ridiculous, Treplyov also utters things which are unquestionably the opinions of Chekhov. Treplyov refers to theater of the day as "deadly scenes and shallow phrases," out of which "they try to fish up a moral—a tiny, comfortable, easy-to-grasp moral, useful for consumptions in the home." By injecting Treplyov with qualities and opinions that Chekhov both valued and ridiculed, he created a character who was not constrained by anyone's morality, including Chekhov's.

Chekhov would insist repeatedly throughout his literary career that he did not judge his characters. He let them be whoever they were, and he had a kind of love for all of them. This disspassionate conception of characters would become quintessentially Chekhovian.

The love lines are set up in the first act. Medvenko is in love with Masha, who is in mourning for her life, in part because she is in love with Treplyov and Treplyov hardly notices her. Treplyov is in love with the actress who performs his play, Nina.

As Treplyov's play quickly breaks up, he is furious about the general lack of respect and attention paid to his work, especially by his mother, Arkadina, who accuses him of being a vain, egotistical little boy. This accusation is full of irony, since she is the most outrageously self-absorbed person in attendance.

Arkadina is escorted by her lover, Trigorin, the famous writer who has accompanied her to her brother's estate. Arkadina introduces Trigorin to Nina, who nearly melts with joy. Trigorin has not only

Arkadina's but Nina's affections also, and Treplyov is left to compete for the attention of both his mother and his muse.

In **Act Two** Arkadina decides she wants to go into town—she claims the country is boring her to death. Shamraev, Sorin's estate manager, refuses to provide the horses to take her. He insists the horses are already occupied hauling rye. The spectacle of servant usurping master is comical, and Sorin does nothing but accept it.

Treplyov appears and offers Nina a dead seagull, one he himself shot, as a sign of his despair that she does not return his love. He tells her, "Soon, in the same way, I shall kill myself." Trigorin, the writer, watches amusedly the whole melodramatic spectacle and takes notes for purposes of exploitation. Nina throws herself at Trigorin, showering him with praise and adulation, but he paints a grim picture of the writer's life for her:

> Day and night one persistent thought obsesses me—I must write, I must write, I must . . . I no sooner finish one story than for some reason or other I must write the next, then a third, and after that a fourth . . . I write endlessly, exactly as relay horses run, and I can't do it differently. So I ask you, what's particularly beautiful or brilliant about that? . . . I have no peace from myself, and I feel that I am consuming my own life. For the sake of the honey that I give away to someone out there, I steal the pollen of my best flowers, pick the flowers themselves, and then trample down their roots.

At the beginning of **Act Three**, Masha declares that she will marry Medvenkeko in order to eradicate her desire for Treplyov. We learn that, between the acts, Treplyov has tried to kill himself but failed and that Arkadina is preparing to leave with Trigorin for the city. Treplyov's suicide attempt is hardly a serious point in the play, since he aimed for his head and missed. When we see him subsequently, he has a bandage wrapped around his head. Everyone, including Arkadina, seems very little concerned about Treplyov, and Trigorin refers to his suicide attempt as "tactless."

Treplyov has a tender moment alone with his mother when at first she gently changes the bandage on his head. The scene quickly turns violent as Treplyov jealously denounces and reviles Trigorin. Here we can see Shakespeare's influence on Chekhov, as he structures a scenario unmistakably reminiscent of Hamlet, who condemned his mother for her recent marriage, which he believed occurred for malignant purposes. Hamlet and his mother, however, unlike Treplyov and Arkadina, had a complicated relationship, at times, very tender.

Arkadina must guard Trigorin from not only Nina but also Treplyov. Right before their departure, Trigorin considers staying in the country, as he has become smitten with Nina, but then he departs in the end after Arkadina desperately pleads with him. At the end of the act, Nina secretly tells Trigorin that she's decided to make a break with her family and become an actress, as she's always dreamed of becoming. She and Trigorin will be reunited soon in the city.

When **Act Four** begins, two years have passed. Masha and Medeveneko are married and have a baby, but Masha is still in love with Treplyov, who has now become a successful writer. Arkadina has been summoned from the city because her brother Sorin is ill. Once again she is escorted by Trigorin. They discuss Treplyov's success as a writer, and Arkadina reveals that she has not read a word he has written, displaying her total self-absorption. Treplyov relays to Dorn the sordid tale of Nina's modest successes in the theater, her affair with Trigorin, the birth and death of their child, and her present destitution.

Nina appears at Treplyov's window presently. She tells him about her trials and her effort to endure. She tells him that she is still in love with Trigorin, who sits playing lotto in the next room with Arkadina and the others from Sorin's estate. Treplyov admits his despair to her:

> I still keep on drifting in a maelstrom of dreams and images, not knowing why it has to be or for whose sake. I don't have faith, and I don't know what my profession is all about.

Here we have the polar opposite of Trigorin, who is driven by his stories. He knows that what he sees and experiences will transmute into one of his stories; life is designed for his purposes. But Treplyov, in his search for new forms, has found that the very idea of new forms is bankrupt. He has learned that one must write and create purely from the soul, without any veneer of imposed purpose. This new knowledge has left him adrift and disillusioned.

He tells this to Nina, who neither understands nor sympathizes. She leaves quickly, rejecting Treplyov's love once again. Treplyov tears up his manuscripts and disappears. We hear a gunshot from off-stage, and Dorn, who is playing lotto with the others, goes quietly to investigate. He returns to announce that a bottle of chemicals exploded in his medicine case. He then takes Trigorin aside and tells him the truth. Treplyov has killed himself.

Treplyov has killed himself because he could not follow Nina's lead. He could not break free of the entrapment of family and familiar surroundings. Though the seagull symbolized Nina as victim, the creature destroyed by Trigorin just for the fun of it, in the end Nina endures, acting and living and loving Trigorin in spite of everything. ❈

List of Characters in
The Seagull

Irina Nikolaevna Arkadina is an actress and the sister of Sorin, on whose estate the play takes place. She is the quintessential primadona, vain and self-absorbed, incessantly listing her stage roles and her best attributes. When her son, Treplyov, puts on an amateur play, she pronounces it "decadent," and when he becomes a famous writer, she secretly concedes that she has never read anything he wrote. She has a ongoing relationship with the famous writer Trigorin, though they are not married and take other lovers from time to time. Within the play, they are a couple.

Konstantin Gavrilovich Treplyov is Arkadina's only son, a very introverted Hamlet-type figure. He is searching artistically for new forms when he stages his symbolist play in Act One. By the end of the last act, however, he has decided that it is not "new forms" which matter per se but writing from the soul. He is in love with Nina throughout the two or so years of the play. She, however, is in love with Trigorin and will not accept Treplyov's love. When he finally believes that he will win her love, she rejects him again, and in the end of the play, he kills himself.

Pytor Nikolaevich Sorin is Arkadina's brother. It is his country estate on which everyone has gathered to visit, commiserate, and fall in love with one another. (The estate itself figures largely in the play: the moon, the lake, the animals.) He is a relatively passive, somewhat comic character who professes not to be able to tolerate country life. His estate manager, Shamraev, completely disregards his orders. Sorin relays that he once wanted two things: to be a writer and to be married. In old age, he is neither.

Nina Mikhaylovna Zarechnaya is a young girl, daughter of a rich landowner near to Sorin's estate and the star of Treplyov's little dramatic effort in Act One. She is also the object of Treplyov's undying love, though she will never reciprocate. Nina falls in love with Trigorin, and when he leaves the estate with Arkadina, she decides to run away to the city and become an actress as she always wanted. During a two-year interval between Act Three and Act Four, she and Trigorin have a child together, the child dies, and Trigorin deserts her. She is the character most identified with the seagull, which Treplyov shoots and gives to her.

Ilya Afansevich Shamraev is a retired lieutenant and Sorin's estate manager. He is a responsible but incorrigibly aggressive manager, making for a rather comedic spectacle when he and Sorin interact. His daughter is Masha, who pines away for Treplyov throughout the play.

Polina Andreevna is Shamraev's wife. She is a minor character, but she continues the chain of unrequited love when she makes a proposal to Dorn, the doctor, who refuses her. She asks him to take her into his home, making it obvious that she too is miserable in matters of love.

Masha is the daughter of Shamraev and Polina. She is hopelessly in love with Treplyov, though he never notices, and she marries Medvedenko, the local school teacher, in an effort to erase Treplyov from her mind, but she does not love him. The marriage does not release her from her attraction to Treplyov, as she had hoped, but she does not give up trying to forget him.

Boris Alekseevich Trigorin is a famous novelist and guest of Arkadina's at Sorin's estate. He is a quiet figure, with an attitude toward his own celebrity much the opposite of Arkadina's. He feels harassed by his own talent and loves to fish in solitude at Sorin's. His liaison with Arkadina is not completely a love relationship but some parts admiration, self-indulgence, and convenience. Trigorin falls in love with Nina on Sorin's estate and engages her in an affair during the two-year interim between Act Three and Act Four. They have a child, the child dies, and Trigorin deserts her, but Nina's love is undying.

Yevgeny Sergeevich Dorn is Sorin's doctor and an ever-present figure amid the group at Sorin's. He is the only one among them who likes Treplyov's play, and he encourages him to persevere in his efforts. He is a counselor-figure to Treplyov, Masha, Sorin, and Arkadina. In the end, he is the one who discovers and conceals from Arkadina the death of Treplyov.

Semyon Semyonovich Medvedenko is a local school teacher and pursues Masha until she consents to marry him. Masha does not love him, however, and she exhibits a minimum of toleration even for his presence. He is a very unflattering portrait of a provincial school teacher, narrow and pretentious. ❁

Critical Views on
The Seagull

ERNEST J. SIMMONS ON THE FIRST PRODUCTION OF
THE SEAGULL

[Ernest J. Simmons has written *English Literature and Culture in Russian; Pushkin; Dostoevsky: The Making of a Novelist; Leo Tolstoy;* and *Russian Fiction and Soviet Ideology.* He is a professor at Columbia University's Russian Institute. In this selection, Simmons gives some history about the first production of *The Seagull.*]

[W]hen the manuscript of *The Sea Gull* encountered difficulties with the censor—mostly over frank expressions of intimate relations between Arkadina and Trigorin—Chekhov entrusted Potapenko with the task of dealing with this official in Petersburg. And in order to meet last-minute objections by the censor, Potapenko, on his own authority, introduced a few slight changes and managed to obtain clearance for the play before the end of August.

An invitation from the Alexandrinsky Theater in Petersburg to stage *The Sea Gull* on October 17 as a benefit performance for the noted comic actress E. I. Levkeeva settled the matter of the opening with Chekhov. It was a fateful decision.

Although the official Theater and Literary Committee approved *The Sea Gull* for performance, its highly critical report might have forewarned Chekhov, if he had had the opportunity to read it, of difficulties ahead. The report stated that the play was a literary effort; that it contained a few characters drawn with refined humor, such as Medvedenko, Sorin, and Shamraev; and that in several scenes it achieved sincere dramatic quality. The report then went on to point out that the play "suffers from substantial defects." Its "symbolism, or more correctly its Ibsenism . . . running through the whole play like a red thread," was sharply condemned as ineffective and unnecessary. Faults were also found in the characterizations of Treplev, Trigorin, Arkadina, and Masha, and a looseness in the structure of the play was criticized.

Certainly the "tons of love," which Chekhov had mentioned to Suvorin, complicating the lives of four women and six men in four separate triangle situations, must have baffled the members of the committee, who were used to relatively simple, conventional plays. With a suicide at the end, they probably wondered why Chekhov described the work as a comedy, for the nontragic frustration that leads Treplev to take his life no doubt evaded them. They sought for the direct appeal and blatant theatricality of typical comedy, and found neither in *The Sea Gull.* Further, their report gives no indication that they perceived the subtleties and nuances of the play or the true significance of its symbolism. Nor is any mention made of the pervasive Hamlet motif, or the indirect appeal of the emotionally evocative dialogue. And the eloquent implications of the silences, the wonderfully effective mood of fused lyricism and wit, as well as the unanticipated truth that emerges from these characters variously disappointed by life, were dramatic innovations beyond the experience of this committee.

Chekhov himself sensed the artistic challenge which *The Sea Gull* would present to a contemporary audience, and at first he was impatient for the trial. One must not be hypnotized by the routine of life, he told Potapenko, who was in raptures over the freshness and originality of the play but worried by its flouting of dramatic conventions. Life was a jumble, Chekhov explained, in which the profound existed along with the trivial, the great with the insignificant, the tragic with the ridiculous, and that was the way it ought to be represented on the stage. And to do this, he declared, echoing Treplev in the play, new forms were needed. After some correspondence with E. M. Karpov, a mediocre dramatist and director of the Alexandrinsky Theater, who sought his approval on casting, Chekhov realized that he must go to Petersburg well in advance of the opening night to discuss these matters and attend rehearsals. "The thirst for fame" drew him to the northern capital, he wrote Leontiev-Shcheglov, and he left for Petersburg on October 7.

The next day Chekhov sat in the dark Alexandrinsky Theater and watched a rehearsal of *The Sea Gull,* the fourth that had taken place. He was mortified by what he saw. Nor did the fifth or sixth rehearsals show any improvement. And at this late point, only five days before the opening, the distinguished but temperamental actress, Mariya Savina, decided that she was unsuited to the role of Nina and rejected it—the very role on which Chekhov thought the whole play depended. In her place stepped the young, dedicated Vera Kommissarzhevskaya, who soon became one of Russia's most celebrated actresses. At that time she was light of build, with large, luminous dark eyes, thin, tense but lovely features, and an extraordinary musical voice.

At the sixth rehearsal Chekhov observed with dismay that several of the cast were absent, a few still read their lines from scripts, and only an assistant director was present to guide the actors. *The Sea Gull* was just another play to them, and it was clear that the limited Karpov, in his staging and instructions to the actors, had failed to understand the structural innovations of the play, its poetic mood, and the tender and refined delineation of character. Shocked by the stilted, traditional intonation of the actors, their false emphasis in reading lines, and their lack of comprehension of the roles they were portraying, Chekhov frequently interrupted the rehearsal to explain the significance of a phrase or discuss the real essence of a characterization. "The chief thing, my dears, is that theatricality is unnecessary," he would repeat. "Really unnecessary. It is entirely simple. They are all simple, ordinary people."

—Ernest J. Simmons, *Chekhov: A Biography* (Boston: Little, Brown and Company, 1962): 365–367.

ROBERT LOUIS JACKSON ON THE IMPORTANCE OF ART IN *THE SEAGULL*

[Robert Louis Jackson is B. E. Bensigner Professor of Slavic Languages and Literatures at Yale University. He is also the President of the International Chekhov Society. His numerous writings include *The Art of Dostoevsky: Deliriums and Nocturnes; The Overwhelming Questions; Reading Chekhov's Text;* and other essays on Turgenev, Gogol, Chekhov, Dostoevsy, and Tolstoy. In this essay, Jackson writes about the centrality of the subject of art in *The Seagull*.]

Art is at the center of *The Seagull*. Four characters in the play are actresses or writers. Everybody talks about art. Everybody embodies or lives out a concept of art. The problem of talent—what it takes and means to become an artist—is a fundamental theme of the play. Illusion and reality, dream and fulfillment in art and life constitute the innermost concern of the author. Finally, art in its most basic form as myth gives expression to the underlying dramatic conflicts and realities in the play: the myth of creation, the Oedipal syndrome and the metaphor of the journey.

In his myth-play in Act I of Chekhov's *The Seagull* the young writer Konstantin Gavrilovich Treplev pictures a bleak future for the world: thousands of centuries have passed and all life has vanished. The bodies of living beings have long ago crumbled into dust, and eternal matter has turned them into stone, water, and clouds; their souls have merged into one. A doleful moon vainly sheds light on this desolation. And desolation it is: "Cold, cold, cold. Empty, empty, empty. Terrible, terrible, terrible."

Konstantin's play itself, as commentators on *The Seagull* have observed, is also terrible. It is a concoction of melodramatic posturing and mannered symbolism. Yet—though bad art—it is, paradoxically, full of Chekhov's art. The action, the character-symbols and portents—all the devices which fail so miserably in Konstantin's play taken by itself and which seem merely a Chekhovian parody of a "decadent" theatrical style—have a distinctly allegorical character in the context of the larger play, *The Seagull*. Just as in Shakespeare's *Hamlet*, so in *The Seagull*, the play within the play reaches out into the psychological drama. But while the import of Hamlet's theatrical is immediately evident, both before and after the performance, the significance of Konstantin's play is only fully apparent by the end of *The Seagull*. Chekhov's use of Konstantin's play is crucial to his whole development of the character of Konstantin and to the expression of some of the central ideas of *The Seagull*. A discussion of Chekhov's play, then, may properly begin with an analysis of the play within the play. ⟨...⟩

> Like a prisoner thrown into an empty, deep well, I do not know where I am or what awaits me. One thing, however, is not concealed from me: in stubborn, savage struggle with the devil, with the element of material forces, I am destined to conquer, and then matter and spirit will unite in a beautiful harmony and the kingdom of the world will is to arrive.

Konstantin's play gives expression to the *pro* and *contra* in his nature. It dramatizes his creative yearnings, the flight of his poetic muse, but in the final analysis it is paradigmatic of the downward spiral of a hopelessly crippled creative spirit. "There's something in it," Dr. Dorn observes after seeing Konstantin's play, something "fresh, naïve." The play, indeed, partakes of poetry, as the audience realizes in Act IV when the young actress Nina Mikhailovna Zarechnaya recites again the opening lines from Konstantin's youthful work. But apart from revealing a propensity for abstractions and symbols ("not a single character that's alive," Trigorin later observes of Konstantin's writings in general), the play discloses Konstantin's tendency toward grandiose dreams and impetuous challenges, on the one hand, and passive retreats and sterile reconciliations on the other. The movement of the play—all appearances to the contrary—is precipitous from self-exaltation to a depressed posture of defeat. Here in his well the poet prophesies "stubborn, savage struggle with the devil" and eventual victory. But this is empty prophecy: the well is dry. The poet himself is inwardly aware of the emptiness of his prophecy, of the utopian character of his mythic dream of "beautiful harmony" and of a "kingdom of world will." He resolves the contradiction between the reality of his nature (his weakness of will, his impotence) and his fantastic dream in the manner of a familiar Chekhovian type.

> But all this will only take place when, little by little, through long, long series of millennia, both the moon, and the bright Sirius, and the earth will turn into dust. And until then, horror, horror.

The "horror" here is, in a sense, an intuition: the self's forereading of its own tragic emptiness.

> —Robert Louis Jackson, "Chekhov's *Seagull*: The Empty Well, the Dry Lake, and the Cold Cave." In *Chekhov: A Collection of Critical Essays,* edited by Robert Louis Jackson (Englewood Cliffs, NJ: Prentice-Hall, 1967): 99–102.

MICHEAL HEIM ON CHEKHOV AND THE MOSCOW ART THEATER

> [Micheal Heim is associate professor of Slavic Languages and Literatures at the University of California at Los Angeles. He is the author of works on Russian drama, intellectual history, eighteenth-century literature, and Czech literature. In this selection, Heim discusses Chekhov's relationship to the Moscow Art Theater.]

Although written several years before the Moscow Art Theater came into existence, *The Seagull* anticipated that Theater's main innovation: its emphasis on ensemble playing or, in negative terms, the abolition of the star system. Chekhov illustrates the vacuity of the star mentality in the persons of Arkadina—who, a star of the second magnitude and slightly past her prime at that, revels in the tributes of provincial students—and Shamrayev, the estate manager, who pesters her with anecdotes of the stars of his generation. He also comes close to suggesting an alternative when Dorin points out optimistically that although the Russian theater may have fewer stars than before, "the average actor has come a long way." But far more important than the lines is the structure underlying them. For Chekhov had written a play that needs no stars, a play that in fact could not be fully appreciated without the kind of principles the Moscow Art Theater stood for.

Who is the "star" of *The Seagull?* At first glance, it is Nina. She is, after all, the title character and the character who undergoes the greatest amount of development during the play. But what about Treplev? In any good melodrama a character who shoots himself is the main character. (Such was the case in *Pashenka*, and such is the case in Chekhov's earlier play, *Ivanov*, which was nothing if not a tour de force for the actor in the title role.) If we place Nina and Treplev on the same level, we cannot leave Arkadina and Trigorin far behind. They are not only essential to the action in their own right; they are to a large extent established, old-guard, passé versions of them.

Each of these artistically oriented couples has a less intense analogous couple. Masha and Medvedenko lead the sort of boring, humdrum existence Treplev might well have forced on Nina. The analogy goes further. Nina has taken her life into her own hands by escaping into the world of the theater; Masha at least breaks away from her parents by marrying Medvedenko. Just as Chekhov refused to offer his audience pat solutions, so he refused to guarantee his characters success, even in their most high-minded undertakings. but when Nina rejects the seagull image in her final meeting with Treplev, when she calls herself an actress, the worst is clearly past. She knows what direction to take and may well develop into precisely the type of actress the Moscow Art Theater had set out to train. (Stanislavskiy and Nemirovich-Danchenko did a good deal of their initial recruiting in provincial theaters like the one Nina is going off to.) Masha's marriage to Medvedenko may not have brought her any relief, but like Nina she has not given up. Medvedenko has accepted a post in another district, and she hopes the change of atmosphere will help her to "tear Treplev out of her heart." And Medvedenko, boor that he is, has the sense to pack up and leave both her family (Shamrayev's petty despotism) and his (the quadruple tyranny of a mother, two sisters, and little brother). One of the main reasons for Treplev's suicide is that he is unable to make just such a move; he is unable to cut off ties with his family, his mother, and strike out on his own.

If Masha and Medvedenko parallel and—to a certain extent—parody Nina and Treplev, then by the same token Polina Andreyevna and Dorn parallel and parody Arkadina and Trigorin. Both women are possessive mistresses; both men are weak-willed lovers of long standing. Both Arkadina and Polina Andreyevna are jealous of Nina, and both are capable of hysterical outbreaks. But while Arkadina gets what she wants (Trigorin goes away with her), Polina Andreyevna does not (Dorn refuses to let her come and live with him).

Structurally, this layered effect gives the play increased depth of characterization. Dramatically, it means that no one character may stand out without upsetting the balance. More than any theater in Russia at the time, the Moscow Art Theater was attuned to maintaining that balance. Identifying with both Nina's quest and Chekhov's talent, it adopted a stylized seagull as its emblem.

>—Michael Heim, "Chekhov and the Moscow Art Theatre." In *Chekhov's Great Plays: A Critical Anthology*, edited by Jean-Pierre Barricelli (New York: New York University Press, 1981): 135–136.

Jerome H. Katsell on Maupassant in *The Seagull*

[Jerome H. Katsell is assistant professor of Russian and Comparative Literature at the University of California at San Diego. He has written about Chekhov, Olesha, and Turgenev. In this essay on *The Seagull*, Katsell focuses on Arkadina's reference to Maupassant's travel sketch, *Sur l'eau,* published in 1888.]

Arkadina refuses to read further in *Sur l'eau* because the Maupassant text describes the actions of society women intent upon capturing and dominating a writer, "the rest is both uninteresting and false," she asserts. The travel sketch then continues to render an account of how such a woman turns a writer into a mere social fixture of her drawing room. It would be well to remember that Dorn, in the presence of Arkadina and Masha, has been reading Maupassant's work *before* the beginning of the second act and that the content of *Sur l'eau* might in fact explain Arkadina's need to demand acknowledgment of her youthfulness, expressed through a display of insecure behavior. She asserts that she never thinks of death, does not look to the future, that she is stylish and careful, and always dressed and groomed, as she puts it, *comme il faut.*

When we turn to the passages Dorn, Masha, and Arkadina have in fact been reading in turn—they must have been at it for some time—we see that the Maupassant text concerns the dangers for a woman of society to become involved with a novelist. There is much about the novelist as described by Maupassant that reminds us of Trigorin, much that might put Arkadina on the defensive about the vulnerability of her position. Here is what Maupassant writes:

> The poet has more delicate charm, the novelist often possesses more wit. But the novelist presents dangers not encountered in the poet—he preys upon, ruins and exploits everything that enters his field of vision. With him there is no tranquility, no assurance that he won't, one day, expose you quite nude [*toute nue*] in the pages of his book. His eye is like a pump that sucks in everything, like the hand of a thief always working away. Nothing escapes him; he ceaselessly amasses and gathers things; he remarks the movements, the gestures, the intentions, everything that occurs about him; he notices the least words, the smallest actions, the least little thing. From morning till night he stores these varied observations of which he creates salable stories, stories that make their way around

the world, which will be read, discussed, and commented on by countless thousands of people. And the most terrible thing of all is that the wretch can't help executing striking portraits, unconsciously, in spite of himself, because he sees things clearly, and he must tell of what he sees. (30–31)

The passage that Arkadina has been reading and listening to, in contrast to the main thrust of the passage read aloud onstage, concerns the power of the writer, his ability to destroy through the use of words, the sense of dominance over others that the novelist's sensitivity and perspicacity give him. She has noticed how Nina reacted to Trigorin—it is probably not the first time the female admiration Trigorin provokes has come to her attention—and now, perhaps, she gets her own back through Masha. The truth of her relationship with Trigorin contained in the passages subsequent to the one read onstage, the ones Arkadina wants to avoid, concerns the woman who, in Maupassant's opinion, neutralizes the writer by her wiles and social position. She draws him into her circle to be admired and shown off, but always under close scrutiny and guard; he becomes the caged literary lion.

If Arkadina does in fact see her portrait in the description of the society woman who must emasculate the novelist in order to control and dominate, it might well help us understand her relationship to Trigorin, and beyond that give us an insight into her relationship to art. Both relationships are intertwined with, and based on, fear. Trigorin must be kept docile, his art not allowed to go beyond his own characterization of it as "charming, talented," but far below the level of a Tolstoy or a Zola. It might be noted parenthetically that Maupassant would neatly fit the description Trigorin applies to himself. This attitude on the part of Arkadina perhaps explains her indulgence of Trigorin's fishing as well as her casual attitude toward his books. She unwittingly allies herself with the middle if not the lowbrow in art, and by the end of the play we see her *offering* gossipy arty talk to Shamrayev.

More important, Arkadina's fear of real art and forms she cannot understand plays into her relationship with Konstantin. There is more than an oedipal relationship here. In view of Arkadina's reaction to the Maupassant passage in the second act, we might reconsider her reaction to Konstantin's play in Act I. His claims to new artistic form in a play that deals with essences and ultimate states of being/nonbeing threaten Arkadina in the potential for power-as-artist that it might portend for Konstantin. She fears the power of potentially genuine art she does not understand in Konstantin. Thus, she rejects the description of the writer's lady who, Maupassant insists, is in danger of finding herself "toute nue" between the pages of a story. There is no indication within *The Seagull*, in fact, that Arkadina *reads* Trigorin. We know that she never reads a word of Konstantin's work after he begins to publish. Could it be that she fears an unflattering portrait of herself in Trigorin's fiction? All the while that she is not supportive of, or interested in, Trigorin's work, she is forcing her own bad art upon him.

> —Jerome H. Katsell, "Chekhov's *The Seagull* and Maupassant's *Sur l'eau*." In *Chekhov's Great Plays: A Critical Anthology*, edited by Jean-Pierre Barricelli (New York: New York University Press, 1981): 19–21.

RICHARD PEACE ON SHAMRAYEV

> [Richard Peace, a professor of Russian language and literature, is head of the Department of Russian Studies at the University of Hull, England. He has written about Dostoevsky, Goncharov, and Gogol. In this selection, Peace discusses the character of Shamrayev and his function within *The Seagull*.]

Masha's father, Shamrayev, serves principally as a figure commenting on Arkadina, but in him he has met her match. Just as she has no money for her son, so he has no horses for her, (or even for his own son-in-law). He tells Arkadina: 'My dear lady! Forgive me, I have the greatest admiration for your talent, I'm prepared to give ten years of my life for you—but I can't let you have the horses.' Like Arkadina he is a capricious despot with a certain 'style', who has a sensitive, but difficult child (Masha) and a partner (Polina) who conducts an *affaire* with another—to this extent the Shamrayev household provides a comic reflection of the relationships of the main protagonists themselves.

Shamrayev's professed veneration of Arkadina's talent always succeeds in devaluing it. He constantly asks her, not about herself, but about other actors—actors, moreover of the past, whom he appears to think she must know. This hardly flatters Arkadina's vanity about her age, and she retorts: 'You're always inquiring about some old fossil or other. How should I know?' The actors he praises are also provincial ones, thus his first words in the play are: 'In 1873, in Poltava, at the fair, her acting was stunning.' The grand airs of Arkadina herself should be seen in this perspective: when, for instance, in Act IV she proclaims her delight with her reception in Kharkov. The trials of a provincial actress are brought out in Nina's words at the end of Act IV (the life has also been described much more starkly in Saltykov-Shchedrin's novel *The Golovlev Family*). There is, perhaps, not as much hope in Nina's career, as some critics wish to see.

Shamrayev combines flattery with a complete lack of tact. Thus his gracious reception of Arkadina in Act IV obviously pleases her, yet it is he, who later in the act will remind Trigorin of the stuffed seagull. In Act I he tactlessly gives expression to the idea which seems to lie behind his praise of older actors:

> SHAMRAYEV: The theatre is in a decline, Irina Nikolayevna. We used to have massive oak trees, now we see nothing but stumps.
> DORN: It's true enough, there aren't so many outstandingly gifted people nowadays—on the other hand, the average actor is much more competent.
> SHAMRAYEV: I can't agree at all with you there. However, it's a matter of taste. *De gustibus aut bene, aut nihil.*

Shamrayev's misquoted tag is, in fact, apt. He wishes to say 'There's no disputing over tastes' (*De gustibus non est disputandum*) but at the same time he manages to imply: 'Speak only good of the dead or say nothing' (*De mortuis aut bene aut nihil*)—a true expression of his own attitude to actors of the past.

Shamrayev's theatrical tittle-tattle relates to the theme of art in a comic way, but at the same time it provides more serious indirect commentary. In Act I Nina tries to elicit Trigorin's reaction to Treplev's play. She is obviously in awe of the famous writer and Arkadina jokingly tells her not to flatter him, as praise causes him confusion. It is then that Shamrayev chooses to tell his story about the Opera Theatre in Moscow, and how the famous bass Silva was praised for a low note by a rural church chorister in a voice a whole octave lower. The story implies that an unknown provincial is capable of outshining the acclaimed professional. The relevance of this to the artistic rivalry of Treplev and Trigorin is further underscored by Chekhov's treatment of the story almost as another 'play within the play.' Not only does Shamrayev act out the chorister's words but his own final comment: 'the theatre just froze' produces an awkward pause on the stage itself. It is only broken by Dorn's pointed remark: 'The angel of silence has flown over us!'

—Richard Peace, *Chekhov: A Study of the Four Major Plays* (New Haven: Yale University Press, 1983): 44–46.

RICHARD GILMAN ON THE CHARACTERS AND THEIR ART

[For a number of years, Richard Gilman was Professor of Drama at Yale School of Drama and he was *Commonweal*'s drama critic from 1961–64. He has written *Chekhov's Plays* and *Modern Drama*. In this selection on *The Seagull*, Gilman discusses Nina and Treployev, their relationships to each other and to their art.]

The Seagull's climactic actions, some of the most passionately unfolding and swiftly revelatory in all of Chekhov, begin with Konstantin in his room, meditating on writing, technique, his own feeling of sterility. The others are playing lotto in an adjoining room. Nina knocks on the French window and when Konstantin brings her in she "puts her head on his breast and sobs quietly," reminding us of Masha's having done the same thing earlier with Dorn.

But once again, as so often in Chekhov, material actions that resemble each other have entirely different aftermaths. From this point on, in Konstantin's and Nina's agitated, discordant, and ultimately "failed" conversation, everything having to do with art and love, talent and the ego, is brought together and we witness what can best be described as the exposure and testing of the two characters' deepest—or rather, since Chekhov isn't interested in depth psychology, their most dramatically representative—selves.

For Konstantin, Nina's reappearance seems to be a miracle; she's come back to save him, he thinks. Earlier he had told his mother,

"She doesn't love me and I can't write any more," but now his hope springs up. Nina is at first bewildered, almost incoherent at times, struggling to express the hard wisdom her recent life has taught her and about which Konstantin knows nothing, despite his possession of the "facts."

"I'm a seagull," she says several times, identifying herself with the bird as victim and with her youth at the lake, and then, "No, that's not right," quickly taking on a real description, not a fictive one—"I'm an actress." And she says to him, still partly under the sway of their easy youthful romance and shared ambitions, "So, you've become a writer. You're a writer, and I'm an actress." Then, in a prologue to the rapid, violent change in attitude she will soon have to him, a movement away from the waywardness of memory and the pull of early desire, she tells him, "I loved you and dreamed of being famous. But now—." The "now" indicates that neither of these things is any longer true and the break leads her to recite a few details of her physical life as an actor. She thus unwittingly baits a trap into which Konstantin will immediately fall.

Ignoring her words and so revealing that his interest in her is selfish and instrumental, a function of his need, Konstantin pours out his misery and persisting desire, telling her that since she left him "life's been unbearable" for him. Then, in the most fateful line in the play, he says to her, "I call out to you, kiss the ground you walked on." To which Nina, "taken aback," responds, "Why does he talk this way?" emphasizing the crisis by saying it again, "Why does he talk this way?"

Nina's use of the impersonal "he" instead of "you" beautifully indicates her sudden understanding of Konstantin's character, so that her "why"s aren't really questions but a recognition and an expression of regret. He has in effect hanged himself by the romanticism that coats her in such sentimental language and by his having pinned his sense of himself as a writer, his vocational ego, to her erstwhile and potential love for him. Early in the play he had engaged in the "she loves me, she loves me not" game with the petals of a flower (in relation to his mother), and this seemingly innocuous activity can be seen in retrospect as a foreshadowing of his fatal lack of emotional maturity.

What Nina regrets or fleetingly mourns is, I think, her loss of innocence in regard to Konstantin, the death of their shared values and beliefs. She has already lost her larger, more comprehensive innocence. In several long, beautifully modulated speeches she traces the course of her spiritual growth. Because of "the worries of love, jealousy" and his "always laugh[ing] at my dreams," her life with Trigorin had made her "petty and small-minded" and her acting had "lost all meaning" and suffered "terribly." But now, she says, "I'm not like I was." Through a process of maturation that Chekhov doesn't describe, and doesn't have to, she has learned to esteem herself and "delight in" her work. Most significant for *The Seagull*'s pervasive themes, she has learned what it means to be an artist.

"I know now, I understand," she tells Konstantin, "that in our work—it doesn't matter whether we act for the stage or write—the most important thing isn't fame or glory, or anything I had dreamed about, but the ability to endure. To know how to bear your cross and have faith . . . when I think about my vocation, I'm not afraid of life."

For all their differences, Nina has come to share with Trigorin an attitude towards what it means to be an artist, or rather towards what it ought not mean.

—Richard Gilman, *Chekhov's Plays: An Opening into Eternity* (New Haven: Yale University Press, 1995): 92–94.

Plot Summary of
Uncle Vanya

Subtitled "Scenes from Country Life in Four Acts," *Uncle Vanya* is the only play of Chekhov's four major plays that he did not label either a comedy or a drama. We are left to discover on our own that it is neither, that it is Chekhov's innovative blend of the two. He had learned after subtitling *The Seagull* "A Comedy in Four Acts," when people often still interpreted it as melodrama, and took a more indirect approach with *Uncle Vanya*, hoping that the elusive tragi-comic quality would manifest itself without imposition.

Like *The Seagull* and *The Cherry Orchard*, it is set on a country estate. Serebryakov, an older retired professor, is the owner, but it was not originally his. The estate was left to him by his first wife, whose death also left him with three dependents: a daughter, Sonya; the deceased wife's mother, Maria Vasilevna; and the deceased wife's brother, Vanya. As the play opens in **Act One**, Astrov, the doctor, sits with the old nurse, Marina, in the garden, relaying his guilt over the death of a patient of his. He is remorseful, because his work is his hope for the future, and in this instance, he has failed. He turns to Marina and asks her:

> Will those people who live after us, in the course of a hundred or two hundred years, those people we're clearing the way for now, will they remember and speak kindly of us? Why, *nyanka*, you know they won't remember.

"People won't remember, but God will," she replies. Again, as in so many of Chekhov's plays, the distant future is an subject of much consideration and desire.

Vanya joins the two of them after a nap and begins his tirade against the professor that will last the length of the play. Vanya has recently been disillusioned by the professor and the importance of his scholarly work.

> For twenty-five years he's gone on chewing up and spitting out everyone else's ideas about realism, naturalism, and every other kind of nonsense. For twenty-five years he's been lecturing and writing what intelligent people have known about for a long time

and what stupid people have no interest in. To put it bluntly, for twenty-five years he's been pouring from one empty pot into the next. And at the same time, what incredible conceit, what cocksure pretensions!

Vanya is not only disillusioned, but he is also envious of the professor's success with women. Specifically, Vanya desires Serebryakov's new, beautiful young wife, Yelena. (The name Yelena, is a form of Helen, which alludes to Helen of Troy.)

Yelena is the object of desire for Astrov also. She is an idle but high-minded young woman, who feels suffocated by her surroundings, both the people and the way of life. Her husband's daughter, Sonya, has been cool toward her because she perceived Yelena's marriage to her father to be about money. Yelena ably refutes this, however, when she and Sonya put past enmity behind them in **Act Two**.

> . . . I swear to you—it was for love that I married him. He fascinated me, as a scholar and a famous person. The love I felt wasn't real. It was artificial, but you see, at the time it seemed very real to me.

But Yelena is faithful to her husband in deed, anyway. Vanya expresses contempt for this sort of fidelity:

> . . . fidelity like hers is false from beginning to end . . . To deceive an old husband you can't endure—that's immoral. To try to suppress your own feelings of life, vitality and youth—that's not immoral.

Yelena feels nothing for Vanya, but she is drawn to Astrov. She and Astrov suppress a potential affair, however. Yelena is fundamentally afraid. She is incapable of action, as are most of the characters in *Uncle Vanya*. Astrov accuses her of infecting everyone with her idleness. She and Serebryakov go about their provincial married lives, and she chokes off what they consider a dishonorable situation.

Telegin, the impoverished landowner, responds to Vanya's condemnation of fidelity with an outrageous story of his almost supernatural devotion to his own wife, who left him the day after their marriage, gave herself to another man, and even had children with him. Telegin is clearly nothing more than a fool.

Astrov is the man of action in *Uncle Vanya*. He is a healer and a protector of the Russian nature. He has a special interest in stopping the devastation of the forests and has even received prizes for his environmental work. He has planted whole forests of trees.

> Only a thoughtless barbarian could burn beauty like this in his stove and destroy what we ourselves can't create. Man is endowed with reason and with the power of creation so he can increase what is given to him, but up to this moment he hasn't created—he's destroyed. The forests diminish year after year, rivers dry up, wildlife is coming to an end . . .

Besides nature, Astrov's other obsession is beauty, thus his attraction to Yelena. Just as the two are intertwined in Astrov's character, the unfulfilled, meddling love that characterizes *Uncle Vanya* is inextricably bound with provincial life. It springs not from genuine feeling, but merely from proximity and boredom.

> I can't bear the life we live, this provincial, boxed-in life in Russia, and I despise it with all my heart and soul. . . . Fate never stops lashing me, there are times I suffer unbearably, and yet there is no light at all in the distance for me . . .

Yelena does not concur with Vanya's criticism of her husband, though she herself is burdened by his pretensions.

> Ivan Petrovich, you're educated and intelligent and you must realize, surely that the world is being destroyed not by plunder or by fire, but by hatred, rancor, and all these tiffs and spats . . .

But Vanya continues his tirade, contending that he has devoted his life to the professor, and now the professor appears to have been a fraud. Vanya had taken on the burden of paying off the estate's debts and sending what was left over to the professor while he was away, doing scholarly work in the city. Vanya's sacrifice was not made without a certain amount of satisfaction, however, since at the time, he thought that the professor was a great man of inestimable value to the world and that his work was gold.

> I took pride in him and his scholarship, I lived and breathed this man. Everything he wrote, every pronouncement he made, seemed to me inspired by genius . . . Dear God, and now? There he is, retired, and the sum total of his life can be seen now? Not one page of his work will remain after he's gone, he's completely unknown, he's nothing!

Vanya feels he has been made a slave to another man. He blames his inconsequential life on the professor, who never asked him for his adoration.

The professor, while not an evil man, is not a hero, thus Vanya feels betrayed. The professor is a pompous old man, with only a feigned purpose and no original insights. Academia seems to be equivalent to nothing for Chekhov, a sort of entombment, causing the professor to be cut off not only from those around him, but from reality.

The professor in *Uncle Vanya* exerts a control over his family, but this control is maintained by the controlled. The victims are willing victims, made complacent by the idleness of country life. Even Vanya confesses this in Act Two when he says, "When there's no real life to live, you must get by with illusions. It's better than nothing after all."

The plot develops in **Act Three** as Sonya confesses her love for Astrov to her stepmother, Yelena. Yelena promises to question Astrov if he returns her love, though Yelena secretly knows that Astrov's constant presence on the estate is because of herself. When Yelena does question him, he accuses her of being coy. He calls her a "bird of prey," and a "beautiful, fluffy weasel."

Serebryakov gathers everyone together to announce that he has made preliminary plans to sell the estate and use the money to buy a *dacha* in Finland. Vanya explodes with anger and venom. He runs off-stage, a shot is heard as he tries to kill himself. Then he runs on-stage and takes aim at the professor. He misses. This hysteria is merely absurd, however.

Yelena decides that she and her husband must leave the estate quickly and permanently. **Act Four** begins with the hasty preparation for their departure. Vanya and Serebryakov agree to be civilized to one another and to carry on with the estate exactly as it has always been. The two of them leave, and subsequently Astrov leaves. Vanya, young Sonya, and Marina are left alone. Chekhov creates an empty, melancholy atmosphere in the end, as Vanya and Sonya begin working immediately, taking accounts of their wares and produce. They tap quietly on the abacus. Telegin plays guitar gently in the background. Vanya and Yelena commiserate. The final monologue is Sonya's as she gives a painful account of their lives, offering a ray of hope for their life after life:

> We shall work for the sake of others, now and when we are old, never knowing peace or rest. And when our own hour has come, we shall die without complaining; . . . We shall see the earthly veils, all our suffering, drowned in mercy that will fill the whole world, and our life will then grow quiet and gentle and sweet as a caress. . . . Uncle Vanya, wait a little while . . . We shall rest. We shall rest!

Sonya's and Vanya's enslavement to the estate is compounded by their unrequited love. Their seemingly petty self-entrapments gain resonance through the obvious breadth of their unhappiness. They are limited people, as limited as the servants who work for them, but they are much more painfully aware of it than the characters of Marina and Telegin. The country, with all of its magnificence and freedom, has enclosed them in a tomb without love. ❃

List of Characters in
Uncle Vanya

Alexandr Vladimirovich Serebryakov is a retired professor, the owner of the country estate on which the play takes place. He is a harmless academic, who has nonetheless, by his very ineffectiveness, wreaked havoc on the lives of those living on his estate. Vanya claims to have wasted his life completely by working without pause for Serebryakov, devoting his life to him. Serebryakov is not a heroic figure, which Vanya has recently realized, and Vanya cannot forgive him for it.

Yelena Andreevna is Serebryakov's young desireable wife, 27 years old. Vanya and Astrov long for her, but she refuses to have an affair with Astrov for her husband's sake, though she no longer loves him. She is an idle figure, relentlessly bored with her country life. She is a shallow person but not altogether ignoble, for she does long for a better life.

Sofya Alexandrovna (Sonya) is Serebryakov's daughter from his first marriage. She is a sensitive, intelligent young girl but not attractive and thus unable to win the attention of the man she loves, Astrov. She, like Astrov, works; she has not succumbed to idleness like everyone else, but this does not lessen her suffering. She is critical of her father's marriage to Yelena, but ultimately she forgives Yelena and sends her on a mission to discover Astrov's feelings for her.

Maria Vasilevna Voynitskaya is the widow of a privy councilor and the mother of Serebryakov's first wife. She lives with them on the estate, and she is idle also. Her favorite pastime is reading pamphlets about feminism. She, like Vanya, has spent a large part of her life working and sacrificing for the professor, but unlike Vanya, she does not resent it.

Ivan Petrovich Voynitsky (Vanya) is Maria Vasilevna's son, brother to the professor's deceased first wife, and uncle to young Sonya. He is a relentlessly unhappy man who feels he once had the potential to be a great man, but that he spent it on the professor, whom he once believed to be a genius. He blames the professor for his own waste, and he ridiculously tries to shoot himself, then the professor, failing both times. The professor's wife, Yelena, is the object of his greatest desire, but she does not reciprocate. In the end, he stays on the estate, doing exactly what he has always done.

Mikhail Lvovich Astrov is a local doctor and a constant presence on Serebryakov's estate. Astrov represents work, as he is normally very busy with his medical practice and with his work conserving the environment. But he has become smitten by Yelena, and recently he spends a good deal of time seeking her company. He accuses her of infecting everyone with her idleness. Though he is drawn to her, he feels no love, because she is too much a creature of appearances.

Ilya Ilich Telegin, also known as Waffles because of his pockmarked face, is an impoverished local landowner and permanent resident on Serebryakov's estate. He is a clownish example of narrow-mindedness.

Marina is an old nurse and long-time nanny to Sonya. She is of the local peasantry and holds a special place in Astrov's heart, as they have known one another for eleven years. She is a good, simple woman but strictly conventional, and she does not understand the hysteria which everyone seems to suffer. ❦

Critical Views on
Uncle Vanya

Nina Andronikova Toumanova on Stanislavsky and Chekhov's Plays

[Princess Nina Andronikova Toumanova was born in Georgia, Russia, but spent the greater part of her life in France. She is descended from Andronikos Komnenos, Emperor of Byzantium (1183–1185). In this chapter, Toumanova discusses Stanislavsky's ideas for the Moscow Art Theater and how Chekhov's plays were the best vehicle for his ideas.]

Constantine Stanislavsky ⟨. . .⟩ conceived of "the realism of the spirit which does not depend primarily upon externals, but which is based on a sincere desire to realize and communicate to the audience the inner realities of the play." Later he was to create his famous "System," which freed the actors from the banality of artificial gestures and bearing and revealed to them the simplicity of artistic perfection. These ideas he shared with Appia and with Gordon Craig, the gifted son of Ellen Terry who was introduced to Stanislavsky by Isadora Duncan and visited him in Moscow in 1911.

For twelve long years Stanislavsky dreamed of the creation of a real theatre based on new principles, but he had no one in whom to confide his thoughts until the summer of 1897, when he met another brilliant man, Vladimir Ivanovich Nemirovich-Danchenko, who taught dramatics in the Philharmonic Society and welcomed every possible chance for reform.

One day they met. Their discussion pertaining to the stage lasted no less than eighteen hours (they met at two o'clock on the afternoon of June 22 and finished at eight o'clock on the morning of June 23). Fortunately they survived, and in that long conversation they decided the fate of what was soon to be the Moscow Art Theatre, destined to play such a tremendous role in the history of Russian civilization and to become "in some ways the most illustrious of all" in the realm of dramatic art. ⟨. . .⟩

The aim of Stanislavsky was "to perfect the illusion in such a way as to make it more and more representative of life." Realism, therefore, was fundamental in his representation, but he believed from the start that "realism which merely copies external aspects does not represent life. There is a hidden, inner psychological realism . . . which is elusive and extremely difficult to attain, but which goes farther than the most faithful reproduction of exterior aspects toward achieving the illusion and the interpretation of life. The aim of the Art Theatre, therefore, has been to produce the mood of a given play . . . more accurately than ever before." Every emotion expressed on the stage had to be psychologically justified. Complete and perfect unity was to be reached by subordinating individual acting to the will of the stage director, who was to make it conform to the general idea of the play. ⟨. . .⟩

Indeed, a new era began for the Russian stage. Following the impulse of the Meininger, Nemirovich and Stanislavsky, not overlooking even the smallest details, became real innovators in the search for a new atmosphere in their theatre. Instead of the irritating bell at the beginning of each act they introduced the gong. Curtains were separated instead of being raised. Lights were subdued to give the effect of cozy and relaxing mellowness. ⟨. . .⟩

The absence of the star system especially suited Chekhov's plays, of which the heroes were not heroes at all, but men and women living with the other characters on terms of touching equality. Nemirovich, a great admirer of Anton Pavlovich, asked for permission to produce *The Sea Gull*, "this marvelous representation of the human soul." Chekhov had an appeal for the actors of the young Theatre as an interpreter of a new form of art built on a profound knowledge of human psychology, the delicate nuances of which were expressed in odd dialogue, in a general slowing down of the speech, in subdued voices, and finally in the creation of that elusive atmosphere which from that time on received the name of mood (*nastroenie*). His dramas gave Stanislavsky a stimulating opportunity to put in practice the theories of the Art Theatre as stated by Nemirovich: "To give back to the stage a living psychology and simple speech. To examine life not only through rising heights and falling abysses but through the every-day life surrounding us. . . . The art of Tchekhov is the art of artistic freedom and artistic truth."

—Nina Andronikova Toumanova, *Anton Chekhov: The Voice of Twilight Russia* (New York: Columbia University Press, 1937): 160–165.

ERIC BENTLEY ON CHEKHOV AND MELODRAMA AND FARCE

[Eric Bentley is a literary critic, translator, and writer on theater. From 1953 to 1969 he was the Brandes-Matthews Professor of Dramatic Literature at Columbia University in New York. He has published numerous dramatic and critical works including: *The Recantation of Galileo Galilei, The Playwright as Thinker, In Search of Theatre, The Theatre of Commitment,* and as editor and translator, *Seven Plays by Bertold Brecht* and *Naked Masks* by Priandello. In this selection, Bentley discusses Chekhov's relationship to melodrama and farce, and how he modified these forms to come up with his own.]

Those who find Chekhov's plays static should read the three early pieces: they are the proof that, if the later Chekhov eschewed certain kinds of action, it was not for lack of dramatic sense in the most popular meaning of the term. Chekhov was born a melodramatist and farceur; only by discipline and development did he become the kind of playwright the world thinks it knows him to be. Not that the later plays are without farcical and melodramatic elements; only a great mimic and caricaturist could have created Waffles and Gaev. As for melodrama, the pistol continues to go off (all but the last of the seven plays have a murder or suicide as climax or pseudo-climax), but the noise is taken further off-stage, literally and figuratively, until in *The Three Sisters* it is "the dim sound of a far-away shot." And *The Cherry Orchard*, the farthest refinement of Chekhov's method, culminates not with the sharp report of a pistol, but with the dull, precise thud of an ax.

These are a few isolated facts, and one might find one hundred others to demonstrate that Chekhov's plays retain a relationship to the cruder forms. ⟨...⟩ Farce and melodrama are not eliminated, but subordinated to a higher art, and have their part in the dialectic of the whole. As melodrama, *The Seagull*, with its tale of the ruined heroine, the glamorous popular novelist, the despairing artist hero, might have appealed to Verdi or Puccini. Even the story of *The Cherry Orchard* (the elegant lady running off to Paris and being abandoned by the object of her grand passion) hardly suggests singularity, highbrowism, or rarefaction.

In the later plays life is seen in softer colors; Chekhov is no longer eager to be the author of a Russian *Hamlet* or *Don Juan*. The homely Uncle Vanya succeeds on the title page the oversuggestive Wood Demon, and Chekhov forgoes the melodrama of a forest fire. Even more revealing: overexplicit themes are deleted. ⟨. . .⟩ Only in the early version does Vanya's mother add to her remark that a certain writer now makes his living by attacking his own former views: "It is very, very typical of our time. Never have people betrayed their convictions with such levity as they do now." Chekhov deletes Vanya's open allusion to the "cursed poisonous irony" of the sophisticated mind. He keeps the substance of Yelena's declaration that "the world perishes not because of murderers and thieves, but from hidden hatred, from hostility among good people, from all those petty squabbles," and deletes the end of the sentence: ". . . unseen by those who call our house a haven of intellectuals." He does not have Yelena explain herself with the remark: "I am an episodic character, mine is a canary's happiness, a women's happiness." ⟨. . .⟩

Chekhov does not tone things down because he is afraid of giving himself away. He is not prim or precious. Restraint is for him as positive an idea as temperance was for the Greeks. In Chekhov the toned-down picture—as I hope the example of *Uncle Vanya* indicates—surpasses the hectic color scheme of melodrama, not only in documentary truth, but also in the deeper truth of poetic vision. And the truth of Chekhov's colors has much to do with the delicacy of his forms. Chekhov once wrote in a letter: "When a man spends the least possible number of movements over some definite action, that is grace"; and one of his critics speaks of a "'trigger' process, the release of enormous forces by some tiny movement." The Chekhovian form as we find it in the final version of *Uncle Vanya* grew from a profound sense of what might be called the *economy* of art.

We have seen how, while this form does not by any means eliminate narrative and suspense, it reintroduces another equally respectable principle of motion—the progress from ignorance to knowledge. Each scene is another stage in our discovery of Chekhov's people and Chekhov's situation; also in their discovering of themselves and their situation (in so far as they are capable of doing so). The apparent casualness of the encounters and discussions on the stage is Chekhov linking himself to "the least possible number of movements." But as there is a "definite action," as "large forces have been brought into play," we are not cheated of drama. The "trigger effect" is as dramatic in its way as the "buried secret" pattern of Sophocles and Ibsen. Of course, there will be people who see the tininess of the movements and do not notice the enormousness of the forces released—who see the trigger-finger move and do not hear the shot. To them, Chekhov remains a mere manufacturer of atmosphere, a mere contriver of nuance. To others he seems a master of dramatic form unsurpassed in modern times.

—Eric Bentley, *In Search of Theater* (New York: Alfred A. Knopf, 1953): 362–364.

Sonia Kovitz on Hopelessness in *Uncle Vanya*

[Sonia Kovitz was assistant professor of Russian language and literature at Lawrence Univerity and is now working in the Ohio State University Library. She has written works on Chekhov, irony, and structuralism. In this essay, Kovitz writes about Chekhov's focus on hopelessness in *Uncle Vanya*.]

Finally you come to a halt, when you realize that you won't have what you want. Or when you get what you want, then you no longer want it: Masha with Kulygin, Yelena with Serebryakov, Andrey with Natasha. Or you no longer know what to want. Astrov is bothered because, as he tells his old nurse, "there is nothing I want, nothing I need, no one I love." Astrov has stepped backward. Uncle Vanya steps forward and kicks the wall he sees before him. "If man will strike, strike through the mask! How can the prisoner reach outside except by thrusting through the wall?" Before firing an (inaccurate) shot at Serebryakov, Uncle Vanya screams while barring his path:

> You have ruined my life! I haven't lived! Thanks to you, I have destroyed, annihilated, the best years of my life. You are my worst enemy!

But Uncle Vanya discovers that it is his own foot that hurts when he kicks the obstacle. Treplev, "cold as if I were living in a dungeon," salutes the wall in true romantic style by shooting himself. The three sisters (or at least two of them, Irina and Ol'ga) want desperately to believe in something beautiful on the other side of the wall, in Moscow. Masha, like Ranevskaya ("oh my sins . . ."), has collided with the wall in full force and goes on loving anyway. It is the same stone wall that Dostoyevskiy's underground man beats upon, and the same that Ippolit (in *The Idiot*) shakes his fist at; he is dying, and he stares out the window at a brick wall. The wall is reality. If this meaningless word means anything, it is whatever you shake your fist at when you can't go any farther; it is what blocks your path. In Chekhov's "Ward No. 6," Andrey Yefimych spends his first night as an inmate imprisoned in the same insane asylum that he had been visiting as a doctor for twenty years:

> Andrey Yefimych walked to the window and looked out at the field. It was growing dark, and on the horizon at the right rose a cold livid moon. Not far from the hospital fence, some two hundred yards, stood a tall white building surrounded by a stone wall. It was the prison.
>
> "So this is reality," thought Andrey Yefimych, and he became terrified. ⟨. . .⟩

Chekhov's plays are about the life journey that sets out for the golden towers of Moscow and arrives instead at the heart of darkness: "idleness, kvas, goose with cabbage, after-dinner naps, base parasitism." The immovable wall of reality, in opening to reveal the abyss, turns into a mirror. By frustrating our desires and forcing us to a halt, it plunges us into the hell of our own nature.

II

*Midway in our life's journey, I went astray
from the straight road and woke to find myself
alone in a dark wood.*
—Dante, *The Inferno*

"You know," says Doctor Astrov, "when you walk through a forest on a dark night, if you see a small light gleaming in the distance, you don't notice your fatigue, the darkness, the thorny branches lashing your face . . . but for me there is no small light in the distance." Astrov's name—from the Greek *astron*, star—says that he is the small gleaming light. But it is a long, hard road to discover that the light is within, which is why you cannot see it in the distance. ⟨. . .⟩

Where Astrov loses heart because he can see no light in the distance, Vershinin consoles himself by imagining one. "Life is hard," he says. "It presents itself to many of us as desolate and hopeless, and yet, one must admit that it keeps getting easier and easier, and the day is not far off when it will be wholly bright." Both men are aware of the stakes in the grim death struggle, but each holds a view of the course of the battle that excuses himself from participating. Here is the guilt of complicity, whether dressed in cynicism or hopeful rhetoric.

> ASTROV: In the whole district there were only two decent, cultured men: you and I. But after some ten years of this contemptible, barbarian existence we have been encompassed by it—it has poisoned our blood with its putrid fumes and we have become just such vulgarians as all the rest.
>
> VERSHININ: At the present time there are only three of your sort in this town, but in generations to come there will be more and more, a time will come when everything will change to your way, people will live like you. . . .

To enter moral combat puts the naked self on the line. Most of Chekhov's characters hide within a mask or shell of ingenious evasions. Vershinin slides either forward or backward in time: "When my little girls were standing in the doorway in their underwear, the street red with the blaze . . . I thought that something of the sort must have happened many years ago, when the enemy made a sudden raid." Astrov, pained by the devastation of the forests, asserts with passion:

> Man is endowed with reason and creative powers, so that he may increase what has been given to him. . . . When I hear the rustling of young trees which I have planted with my own hands, I realize that the climate is somewhat in my power.

But in his own life Astrov will recognize no such power. To Uncle Vanya's weeping, "to begin a new life . . . tell me how to begin," he replies sharply: "Oh, come now! What sort of new life can there be! Our situation—yours and mine—is hopeless."

> —Sonia Kovitz, "A Fine Day to Hang Oneself: On Chekhov's Plays." In *Chekhov's Great Plays: A Critical Anthology*, edited by Jean-Pierre Barricelli (New York: New York University Press, 1981): 189–192.

Irina Kirk on *Uncle Vanya* and Beauty

[Irina Kirk is Professor of Comparative and Russian Literature at University of Connecticut. She has published *Dostoevsky and Camus* and *Profiles in Russian Resistance*, as well as a novel, *Born with the Dead*. In this chapter, Kirk writes about the theme of beauty in *Uncle Vanya*.]

The two central images embodying physical beauty are the Russian forests and Elena. The idealistic Dr. Astrov plants new trees every year because, as Sonya says:

> He claims that forests beautify the earth, and so teach man to understand the beautiful, and instill in him a feeling of respect and awe. Forests temper the severity of the climate. In countries where the climate is warmer, less energy is wasted on the struggle with nature and that is why man there is more gentle and loving; the people there are beautiful, supple, and sensitive, their speech is refined and their movements graceful.

Astrov believes that man's creative and rational powers should be devoted to the preservation of that which is aesthetic in the environment, so that in a thousand years' time the earth might still retain its loveliness.

On the other hand, Vanya has a cynical attitude toward the preservation of forests. He is much more interested in the utility of the trees on his estate than in their beauty, and feels no compunction in burning logs in his fireplace or using wood for his barns. This attitude is not surprising in view of his physical appearance, which is described as "disheveled."

Both Astrov and Voinitsky are united in their love for the beautiful Elena. When Astrov realizes that he is infatuated with Elena he abandons his forest and medical practice to "seek her out greedily." Yet Astrov's tragedy is that while his attraction to Elena reveals his lack of a personal life, it does not involve his emotions. At the beginning of the play he says, "I don't love anyone," and this becomes the leitmotif which is confirmed in the last scene. His parting kiss to Elena is one neither of love nor of passion, but simply a gesture toward a momentarily aroused feeling that at one time in his life could have been real. Astrov's nature, as indicated by his desire to heal and to preserve the beauty of forests, is creative, yet he fails in the design of his own life.

Apparently Stanislavsky did not understand that point, for in his letter to Olga Knipper Chekhov writes in regard to the last scene:

> In accordance with your orders I hasten to reply to your letter where you ask about the last scene of Astrov and Elena. You write that Astrov in that scene behaves with Elena as with someone madly in love, that he clutches at his feeling as a drowning man for straw. But this is incorrect, completely incorrect. Astrov likes Elena, she overwhelms him with her beauty, but in the last act he already knows that nothing will come of it, that Elena will disappear from him forever—and he talks with her in this last scene in the same tone of voice as the heat of Africa, and kisses her, just simply out of nothing to do. If Astrov plays this scene violently, then the entire mood of the fourth act will be destroyed. (September 30, 1899)

In opposition to Astrov's character, Uncle Vanya could perhaps be called destructive. Astrov accuses him of harboring this quality in respect to the forests, and Elena remarks on it in regard to other people:

> As Astrov said just now, see how thoughtlessly you destroy the forests, so that soon there will be nothing left on earth. In just the same way you recklessly destroy human beings, and soon, thanks to you, loyalty and purity and self-sacrifice will have vanished along with the woods. Why can't you look with calm indifference at a woman unless she belongs to you? Because . . . the doctor is right. You are all possessed by a devil of destructiveness; you have no feeling, no, not even pity, for either the woods or the birds or women, or for one another.

Yet just as Astrov fails to create, Uncle Vanya does not succeed in culminating his destructive impulses. He has already sacrificed the greater part of his life in a false dedication to the professor, who is a fraud. When Vanya becomes aware of the implications of his wasted life he attempts to shoot the professor and then himself. Both times he fails, and as a further insult to his masochistic pride, no one attempts to arrest him. Uncle Vanya is denied even the comfort of being thought of as a madman or a potential murderer; he is just a jester, devoid of any distinguishing personal trait. In his failure to destroy lies his inability ultimately to act out anything at all.

Uncle Vanya does not arouse anyone's sympathy. There is something comic in his love for Elena and in his homely dreams of a mediocre life with her. It is also obvious that while Elena responds to Astrov as a man, she does not to Uncle Vanya. Elena succeeds in resisting the temptation to consummate her attraction to Astrov, but in the best Freudian fashion takes his pencil as a souvenir of the possibility of an affair.

Astrov is said to be Chekhov's favorite character. Indeed, he is close to Chekhov in the lack of sentimentality with which he treats his profession as a doctor, in his lack of illusions, in his interest in alleviating the ills of Russia, in his desire to preserve the beauty in the world, and his uncommitted personal life. (Chekhov wrote *Uncle Vanya* before he married Olga Knipper.)

—Irina Kirk, *Anton Chekhov* (Boston: Twayne Publishers, 1981): 139–141.

GARY SAUL MORSON ON YELENA AND WORK

[Gary Saul Morson was born in 1948 in New York City. He is the Frances Hooper Professor of Arts and Humanities and Professor of Slavic Languages at Northwestern University. He is author of *The Boundaries of Genre: Dostoevsky's "Diary of a Writer" and the Traditions of Literary Utopia; Hidden in Plain View: Narrative and Creative Potentials in "War and Peace"*; and other works on Chekhov, Turgenev, and Bahktin. In this essay on *Uncle Vanya*, Morson focuses on the character of Yelena (Elena) and her attitude toward work.]

Elena does not work but, rather, as Astrov observes, infects everyone around her with her idleness. The old nurse speaks correctly when she complains that many of the household's ills derive from the visitors' disruption of old habits, habits related to work. A schedule, arrived at over the course of decades and carefully calibrated so that the estate can be well managed, has been replaced by a purely whimsical approach to time: Marina is awakened to get the samovar ready at 1:30 in the morning.

The *intelligentsia* may view habits as numbing, but from the standpoint of prosaics, good or bad habits more than anything else shape a life. Attention, after all, is a limited resource, and most of what we do occurs when we are concentrating on something else or on nothing in particular, as the sort of action and dialogue in Chekhov's plays makes clear. And yet it is the cumulative effect of all those actions, governed largely by habit, that conditions and indeed constitutes our lives. Moreover, habits result from countless earlier decisions and therefore can serve as a good index to a person's values and past behavior. That, indeed, is one reason Chekhov emphasizes them so much and one way in which he makes even short literary forms so resonant with incidents not directly described. Chekhov's wiser characters also understand that attention can be applied to new problems that demand more than habit only if good habits efficiently handle routine concerns. They keep one's mental hands free.

Relying on beauty, charm, and high ideals—she really has them—Elena does not appreciate the importance of habits, routine, and work. For her, life becomes meaningful at times of high drama, great sacrifice, or passionate romance. That is to say, it can be redeemed only by exceptional moments. Consequently, when those moments pass, she can only be bored. Sonya tries to suggest a different view. She values daily work and unexceptional moments, but Elena cannot understand:

> ELENA ANDREEVNA: [*in misery*] I'm dying of boredom, I don't know what to do.
> SONYA [*shrugging her shoulders*]: Isn't there plenty to do? If you only wanted to . . .
> ELENA ANDREEVNA: For instance?
> SONYA : You could help with running the estate, teach, take care of the sick. Isn't that enough? When you and Papa were not here, Uncle Vanya and I used to go to market ourselves to sell the flour.
> ELENA ANDREEVNA: I don't know how to do such things. And it's not interesting. Only in idealistic novels do people teach and doctor the peasants, and how can I, for no reason whatever, suddenly start teaching and looking after the peasants?
> SONYA : I don't see how one can help doing it. Wait a bit, you'll get accustomed to it. [*Embraces her*] Don't be bored, darling.

Elena significantly misunderstands Sonya. Given her usual ways of thinking in literary terms, she translates Sonya's recommendations into a speech from an "idealistic novel." That, presumably, is why she ignores the possibility of helping with the estate and singles out teaching or doctoring the peasants. She imagines that Sonya offers only a ridiculous populist idyll.

If that were what Sonya meant, Elena's objections would be quite apt. Her misunderstanding allows Chekhov to make a characteristically prosaic point about meaningful activity. In the Russian countertradition, the dynamics and significance of work—daily, ordinary work—figure as a major theme. Elena's only idea of work corresponds to a view that Levin learns to reject in *Anna Karenina*—work "for all humanity"—and she correctly rejects that choice as work "for no reason whatever." What she cannot understand is the possibility of a different sort of work that would be meaningful: prosaic work.

Thinking like a member of the *intelligentsia*, she believes that either meaning is grand and transcendent or else it is absent. Her mistake in marrying the professor has convinced her that transcendent meaning is an illusion, and so she, like Voinitsky, can imagine only the opposite, a meaningless world of empty routine extending endlessly. But Sonya's actual recommendation, like the sort of daily work Levin describes as "incontestably necessary," implicitly challenges the very terms of Elena's, and the *intelligentsia*'s, dialectic.

Sonya recommends taking care of the estate *because it has to be done*. She can draw an "incontestable" connection between getting the right price for flour and making the estate operate profitably or between not allowing the hay to rot and not indulging in waste, which is troubling in itself. Like Tolstoy, Chekhov had utter contempt for the *intelligentsia*'s (and aristocracy's) disdain of efficiency, profitability, and the sort of deliberate calculation needed to avoid waste. That is one reason the play ends with the long-delayed recording of prices for agricultural products.

When Elena characterizes caring for peasants as a purely literary pose, Sonya replies that she does not see "how one can help doing it." For Sonya, it is not a literary pose, and it serves no ideology but is part of her more general habits of caring for everyone. High ideals or broad social goals have nothing to do with her efforts on behalf of others, as we see in this very passage when she responds not with a counterargument but with a sympathetic embrace of the despairing Elena.

Sonya understands that both work and care require habits of working and caring. One has to know how they are done, and they cannot just be picked up "suddenly," as Elena correctly observes. Elena has the wrong habits, and that is her real problem. What she does not see is that she needs to begin acquiring new ones, which is what Sonya is really recommending.

—Gary Saul Morson, "*Uncle Vanya* as Prosaic Metadrama." In *Reading Chekhov's Text*, edited by Robert Louis Jackson (Evanston, Ill.: Northwestern University Press, 1993): 222–224.

RICHARD GILMAN ON THE CHARACTERS' HOPE FOR A BETTER LIFE

[For a number of years, Richard Gilman was Professor of Drama at Yale School of Drama and he was *Commonweal*'s drama critic from 1961–64. He has written *Chekhov's Plays* and *Modern Drama*. In this selection on *Uncle Vanya*, Gilman discusses Chekhov's characters' faith in the future and hope for a better life.]

Astrov himself, Vanya, and Yelena, despite their various moral or psychic afflictions—dilemmas is a better word—are appealing, sometimes wise; most of all they're substantial. Sonya is full of a rough sort of charm, innocent at first and then marked by sorrow. Telegin, for all his timidity and seemingly irrelevant stories (perhaps because of them), touches us. Marina is the old mothering nurse we'd all like to have had. Even Serebryakov, pompous and hypochondriacal as he may be, is far from contemptible. Only Vanya's mother, forever scribbling in the margins, can be said to be wearisome, which is why Chekhov strategically keeps her off at the dramatic edges, having her stick her nose in only once in a great while, a note of tiresomeness and banal rectitude.

Why then do so many of the characters complain about being "stuck" with each other and in this place? To answer this we have to take up some other questions first. Why do so many Chekhov characters reverse the myth of a Golden Age, installing it in the future? ⟨. . .⟩ And why do so many younger figures manage their lives in a constant draining fever of expectations, hopes, reveries about "tomorrow," next year, next year in Moscow? From "A Visit": "White, wan, slender and very beautiful in the moonlight, she was expecting tenderness; her constant dreams of happiness and love had exhausted her."

How often in Chekhov do people imagine the future, near or far, as splendid, full of wishes granted? "A new life will dawn one day," says a character in the remarkable long story "Ward Six," "and justice will triumph. . . . I may not live to see it . . . but someone's grandchildren will." And from "A Visit": "She was making plans for the future . . . and this life, when she was working and helping others, seemed wonderful and poetic to her." Time to come: imminent or remote, but either way transfigured, a promise kept. But by whom, to whom?

Chekhov once wrote in a letter a most disturbing line, enigmatic at first but quickly opening up its meaning: "I call peering into the future by no other name but cowardice." How are we to take this? Chekhov wasn't absurdly saying that we ought never to plan, or look ahead when necessary or even when not; he wasn't advocating immobility or that we avert our eyes from everything but the moment. The key words in the sentence are "peering into," with their suggestion of eavesdropping, looking through a transom, craning over the top of the actual world to gaze on a presumably different reality. The itch to know about time to come in "ordinary" people, that's to say those without professional or scientific interest in the future, without formal status as prophets, is a mark of restlessness, disgruntlement, or sterile dreaming.

Chekhov's "cowards," his people who so ineffectually, if understandably, try to occupy the future, who practice, charmingly sometimes, or earnestly or windily, this barren farsightedness, in that way displace their discontents, projecting them onto time to come, for absolution, transfiguration, or simply relief. They wish to know, to find out (Olga's "If we could only know" why we suffer) or to be elsewhere (Moscow as the future) or to become someone else ("If

I were to be born two hundred years [from now], I'd be a different [better] man," from "Ward Six"); or they anticipate, like Astrov, that time to come will chastise present delinquencies, or, like Vershinin in *Three Sisters*, that it will supplant present sorrow.

And then they are forced back from their temporary and forgivable pusillanimity by the way the plays work. They are stuck, though not in remediable circumstances; they're where they are, not elsewhere, they're who they are, not other beings, and they have to live through this life. Like Beckett's characters in urns, in a heap of sand, on a lonely road at evening, or like the Unnamable inching through the ooze, they're within time where, because of the secret pact among the tenses, it's always too early or too late. ⟨T⟩he Prozorov sisters don't get to Moscow because *Three Sisters* is about their not getting there. In the same way, through painfully arrived at recognitions the characters of *Uncle Vanya* will know themselves to be in a drama about how it is, now. ⟨. . .⟩

It's true that the complaint against the way things are is, in Chekhov's work, directed against circumstances, material ones; the despoliation of the forests and countryside in *Uncle Vanya* is real enough, the constrictions of provincial life are not to be denied. But, we have to think, what would prosperity do for these people? What would it mean for them to be part of a scintillating society, or to have "satisfying" careers? How would a transformation of their local world redeem them? We should remember how, in *Ivanov*, Nikolai curtly dismisses Lebedev's well-meant suggestion that "your environment's got you down" with "That's silly, and it's been said before." It's a cliché of social and situational analysis. Nikolai's true anguish, like that of all Chekhov sufferers, is ontological, mysterious, a matter of the structures of existence out of the reach of therapy or civic planning. Sociological interpreters of Chekhov will always reject this, and ideologues will deny it too, as from a different perspective deconstructionists scorn the notion of any permanence in human nature, any perennial condition of the self.

In a profound irony the Soviets chiefly celebrated Chekhov as a literary forerunner, seeing him, the way Gorky did, as an accurate portraitist of the grayness and misery of life, the injustice of it, but stressing that this was the way it was under the *tsarist* system; they regarded expressions of yearning for the future by

Chekhov characters as a yearning toward the Soviet state. "Surely we can feel in 'The Steppe,'" Yermilov writes, "the breath of the fresh wind of the heroic life which was one day to triumph in our country!" And this biographer-critic mourns Chekhov's ignorance of the Marxist movement that was starting to assert itself in the nineties.

Chekhov wasn't ignorant of Marxists. He despised them as he did all narrow, future-crazed fanatics; in a letter from Nice in the winter of 1896–97 he said that one pleasure in being away from Russia was that he didn't have to see "Marxists with their arrogant physiognomies." With the steadiest of eyes on the present, he stayed with what he saw and could imagine, offering no solutions and giving his contemporaries their own lives, gray and miserable or not, simply theirs, at the same time as he gives us, as Shaw said of Ibsen, "ourselves in our own situations." One of those situations is perpetual loss, the grief of the actual.

> —Richard Gilman, *Chekhov's Plays: An Opening into Eternity* (New Haven: Yale University Press, 1995): 118–121.

Plot Summary of
The Three Sisters

The Three Sisters is the only one of Chekhov's four major plays he subtitled, "A Drama," and it is undoubtedly the one most permeated by an atmosphere of ruin and death. Specifically, it is the character of Natasha who brings destruction to the Prozorov household, where the three sisters, Masha, Irina, and Olga, along with their brother Andrey, live together. Natasha gradually, almost imperceptibly, over the course of the play evicts the Prozorov sisters from their home. In Act One, Natasha is Andrey's fiancée. By Act Two, she is his wife. In Act Three, she asserts herself as the head of the household, and by the end of the play she has managed to edge the three sisters completely out of the house.

It is her seeming harmlessness that causes the Prozorovs to fall prey to her. She takes care that her children have the best rooms, forcing Irina and Olga to share a room. Then Olga is promoted to principal at her school and must move into the school itself. Irina, who is a telegraph operator at the start of the play, acquires her teaching certificate and will undoubtedly have a similar fate.

Again Chekhov overlays the plot with an elaborate web of small tedium and every-day life: idle conversation, afternoon tea, unfulfilled desires, distant music, quietude, and sleepiness. Chekhov strives to depict the large events of life in the smallest way possible. In Act Three, for example, while a portion of the town burns to the ground, alarms ringing off in the distance, the Prozorov household is staged as silent and subdued.

As always, Chekhov's characters obsess about the future, where they believe life will be renewed in beauty and hope. For the three sisters, Moscow represents the future as well as the past. They remember it with enormous longing and affection, for they were Muscovites themselves in their early youth. Their father, an army colonel, was transferred to the town in which they now reside eleven years ago, and they have been striving to return to Moscow, ever more urgently, since that time. "To Moscow, to Moscow!" is a refrain throughout the play, the expression that most defines the three sisters.

As the play opens in **Act One**, Irina, dressed in a white dress, is having her name-day party. It is a celebration tinged with death, however, since it is the one-year anniversary of their father's death as well. Many of the town's high-ranking military are there to honor Irina on her name-day, but the atmosphere is certainly not one of jubilation. Tuzenbakh, a lieutenant, and Solyony, a captain, are present, when Chebutykin, the army doctor, presents Irina with a silver samovar as a present. This is a rather embarrassing and inappropriate present, however, since it is traditionally the type of gift presented on a silver wedding anniversary. Chebutykin admits freely that he was once in love with the sisters' deceased mother.

Vershinin, a lieutenant-colonel battery commander from Moscow, is a newcomer to the town who is introduced at the party. He knew the sisters' father and remembers the three sisters as little girls. He is drawn particularly to Masha, who always wears black, and an affair develops shortly, in spite of Vershinin's wife and his little girls—and in spite of Masha's husband Kulygin. Kulygin is a school teacher who married Masha when she was eighteen, Masha having been taken by his apparent sophistication. But his cleverness was just an illusion supported by her own youth and ignorance, and she now knows it. Masha and Vershinin know true happiness in their brief affair, but by the end of the play, Vershinin will return to Moscow, along with most of the battery, and the sisters will be left behind and alone.

Vershinin and Tuzenbakh begin a dialogue about the future, which will appear intermittently throughout the play. The two characters represent hope and despair, respectively, though experientially it is Vershinin who suffers and Tuzenbakh who achieves a measure of contentment. Tuzenbakh believes that in the future "life itself will remain very much the same as before, a hard life, full of secrets and happiness. And a thousand years from now, man will be sighing much the same as before, 'Ah, how difficult life is!'" Vershinin believes the opposite. He is the voice of optimism and change:

> In the course of two hundred, three hundred, or even a thousand years—the length of time doesn't matter—a new, a happy life will appear. We won't share in this new life, of course, but we're living for it, we're working for it, yes, even suffering for it. We are creating that new life now. That's the sole purpose, the reason for our existence, and if you'd like, for our own happiness . . . there isn't going to be any happiness for us, there shouldn't be, and there won't be, not for us . . . The only thing we must do is to work and keep on working.

"According to you, no one must even dream of happiness! But what if I am happy!" demands Tuzenbakh. Vershinin's approach to this contradiction is simple: "you're not."

The sisters have suffered without satisfaction. They have only the vision of Moscow to comfort them. Irina states their case:

> We three sisters certainly haven't found life either fine or beautiful up to now, life has devoured us like weeds in the garden . . . I'm starting to cry. . . . I should work, work. That's the reason we're unhappy, the reason we see life as dark and dreary. It's because we've never known what it is to work. We were born of people who despised work.

Work for the sake of work is a central theme in *The Three Sisters*. Except for Chebutykin and the antagonist, Natasha, all the characters crave work in some way. They revile idleness, even if they participate in it. Tuzenbakh foresees a change in the Russian way of life:

> The time has come, something huge and immense is coming nearer and nearer to all of us—a strong, exhilarating storm is beginning to gather . . . a storm will soon cleanse our whole society—sweep away all the laziness, the indifference, the prejudice against work, the rotten boredom.

Considering the imminence of the 1917 revolution, this is a remarkable vision Chekhov gave to Tuzenbakh. Characteristically, however, Chekhov provides an indictment of the working class to accompany this fresh vision, leaving the audience without a clear position.

Natasha is the representative of base utilitarianism. She enters for the first time wearing a pink dress with a green belt. (Costume is particularly important in this play.) Olga, the oldest sister, who wears the navy-blue uniform of a school teacher, comments immediately on Natasha's vulgar clothing, "You are wearing a green belt! My dear, it's not right!"

At this point, Natasha is merely Andrey's girlfriend, and the sisters refuse to believe that their brother would seriously consider marriage to this commoner. By the end of Act One, however Andrey proposes and before the beginning of **Act Two**, they have married and had a child.

Olga, the sister who lives most in her memories, is resigned to a modest life of work as a teacher; she represents duty and the positive aspect of the cultured class. She, along with her sisters, symbolize what will be lost if life becomes merely work and nothing else. "Every sort of rudeness, even the slightest, even a tasteless work, pulls me apart inside . . ." she comments to Natasha when Natasha chastises their faithful servant Anfisa for no good reason.

Andrey is indirectly the source of destruction, while Natasha is the direct source. Andrey is a talented man who seems to purposely sink into mediocrity and then dreams of the greatness he once had the opportunity to attain. His father had intended him to have a university career in Moscow, but upon the death of his father, he threw off this ambition as quickly as possible. He marries Natasha, a small and petty woman whose main concern is obtaining a comfortable bourgeois life, specifically the Prozorov home. She is cruel and ruthless and the general passivity and malaise of the Prozorov siblings leaves them vulnerable to her perfidiousness.

By Act Two however, Andrey is regretting everything already:

> Dear God in heaven, I am secretary at the District Council, the very same Council where Protopopov presides, I am secretary, and the most I can hope for, the very most is to become a member of the District Council myself . . . me who dreams every night that I am a professor at the Moscow University, a famous scholar of whom all Russia is proud!

He seems to have forgotten that he gave up the opportunity willingly. He allows Natasha into the house and she, representing coarse, uncultured small-mindedness, will soon take over. First, she asks for Irina's room for her baby; Irina does not put up a fight.

Irina has two prospects of marriage that could potentially save her from an empty future, but she loves neither of them. The bombastic Tuzenbakh and the withdrawn Solyony both love her, while she becomes older and less spirited with each passing Act. She will consent to marry Tuzenbakh by the end of the play, but he will be killed in a duel with Solyony.

By the end of the second act, both Solyony and Tuzenbakh have confessed their love for Irina; Solyony has declared that he would kill anyone who tried to rival him; Natasha has begun an affair with Protopopov, the head of the council on which Andrey sits; and Andrey has deteriorated even further, gambling away hundreds of rubles.

In **Act Three** Natasha declares aloud that, "I—am in charge of the house." A fire erupts in town between Act Two and Act Three and in the distance we hear the alarm bells striking. The Prozorov household is safe from the fire literally but not metaphorically. Vershinin's household has been badly damaged by the fire, however, and he expresses a profound tenderness for his two little girls, which is to say, for innocence: "I kept thinking the very same thought—what more must they still live through on this earth."

Act Three also contains the first admission by one of the sisters, Irina, that they will never see Moscow. She loses heart and sinks into despair. She was holding out for Moscow to find her true love. By the end of the third act Irina finds out that the brigade will be sent away and all their beloved officers will disappear, so she consents to marry Tuzenbakh.

Act Four, set outside the house itself, begins with farewells. Irina is joyful that she will be leaving with the brigade until Tuzenbakh is killed off-stage by Solyony. Olga has moved into the school now that she is headmistress. Natasha orders all the fir trees on the land cut down, and she tells Irina, in an ironic reversal, that the belt she wears does not suit her at all. The brigade leaves and Olga has the last words, "If only we knew, if only we knew." Only Anfisa, the simple servant is happy and satisfied with her lot. *The Three Sisters* is a soft, gentle lullabye into decay and despair. ❀

List of Characters in
The Three Sisters

Olga Prozorov is the oldest sister. She is 28 years old and she is a school teacher, always wearing the dark blue uniform of a civil servant. She is unmarried and will probably never marry. She longs for Moscow and lives in her memories of their life there.

Masha is the middle sister, and for her nothing is right. She was married to Kulygin when she was very young, at which time she thought he was exceptional. She no longer does, however, and is not happy in her marriage. During the course of the play, she engages in an affair with Vershinin. Her love for Vershinin is real. In the last act the officers all leave town, including Vershinin—and he is gone forever.

Irina is the youngest sister and she is sought after by two officers who engage in a duel toward the end of the play. Irina finally accepts a proposal of marriage from one of the men, Tuzenbach, but he is killed in this duel. She is the most hopeful and ebullient sister at the beginning of the play, but she gradually loses spirit and hope, finally admitting aloud that they will never make it to Moscow.

Andrey Sergeevich is brother to the three sisters. He is talented man, intelligent and musical, who was intended to have a university career in Moscow. When his father died approximately a year before the beginning of the play, Andrey threw away the ambitions he percieved to be his father's rather than his own, but by the end of the play he is merely a small petty councilman and a gambler—and he knows it. His marriage to Natasha in particular has ruined him.

Natalya Ivanovna (Natasha) is Andrey's fiancée in the first act, and later his wife. She is the primary source of ruin and destruction in the play, though the Prozorov siblings are not blameless in their passivity toward her. She is common and grasping, and the sisters consider her beneath them. She is without refinement of manners or taste and is needlessly cruel to the servant Anfisa.

Fyodor Ilich Kulygin, a school teacher, is married to Masha. Masha was eighteen when they married and she was enamoured of his great wisdom and learning. She is no longer in love with him, however, and finds him tedious. When Masha engages Vershinin in an affair, he pretends not to notice and even restates his love for her.

Alexandr Ignatevich Vershinin, a lieutenant-colonel battery commander, has arrived recently in town from Moscow with his wife and two little girls. He is presented at Irina's name-day party, where he meets Masha, with whom he has a love affair. Vershinin's great hope is for the future generations who will benefit from toil and work in the present. In the end, he and his battery leave town.

Baron Nikolay Lvovich Tuzenbakh, a lieutenant, is a long-time friend of the Prozorovs and suitor of Irina's, though Irina does not return his love. He is willing to marry her in spite of this, however, as he is realist who is easily satisfied. Tuzenbakh does not believe in the future. He believes everything will remain the same, and he professes, unlike any of the other characters except Anfisa, to be happy now. In the end, he is killed in a duel with Solyony.

Captain Vasily Vasilevich Solyony, shy and morose, can barely tolerate Tuzenbakh. He is very argumentative and declares early in the play that he will kill any rival for Irina.

Ivan Romanovich Chebutykin, an army doctor, is a long-time friend of the Prozorovs. He was once in love with the deceased mother and embarrasses Irina by giving her a silver samovar for her name-day. This was a silver anniversary present, not appropriate for a name-day. Chebutykin is an alchoholic with a most nihilistic attitude toward life. "Nothing matters" is his frequent refrain. This attitude can be traced in part to his guilt over a patient he feels that he killed.

Alexey Petrovich Fedotik, a second lieutenant, is a frequent visitor to the Prozorov househould. He and Rode bring flowers for Irina's name-day. He also presents Irina with a spinning top, a children's toy. This bauble represents their lives, their predicament.

Vladimir Karlovich Rode, a second lieutenant, also teaches gymnastics at the high school. He is a visitor to the Prozorovs. He and Fedotik bring flowers for Irina's name-day.

Ferapont, a watchman from the District Council, is an old man. He is the messenger for Protopopov, who is a large, though off-stage presence in the play. Protopopov is the head of the District Council and becomes Natasha's lover, becoming a source of strife and humiliation for the sisters and particularly for Andrey. Ferapont is Protopopov's representative, though he is a mild-mannered, harmless old man.

Anfisa, an old nurse of eighty years, has been with the Prozorovs for their whole life. She is a simple servant woman who is satisfied with little. Natasha abuses her badly when she becomes head of the household. In the end, Anfisa joins Olga at the school, but she does not lament her departure from the Prozorov house. Instead, she is amazed at her luck that she has always been comfortable and provided for. ❊

Critical Views on
The Three Sisters

W. H. Bruford on Chekhov and Religion

[W. H. Bruford, professor of German at the University of Edinburgh, has written *Germany in the Eighteenth Century*, *Theatre, Drama and Audience in Goethe's Germany*, and *Some German Memories*. Here, Bruford discusses Chekhov's relationship to religion and his hopeful vision of a secular world.]

If we ask what kind of truth Chekhov contemplates as the goal of man's efforts, it is clear from *The three sisters*, *The cherry orchard* or his last published story, *Betrothed*, that it is an entirely secular one. He looks forward to a state of things when the moral sciences will have caught up with and been co-ordinated with the natural sciences, and a society can be established in which men will be delivered from want, injustice and fear. 'Everything in the town had grown old, out of date, and was only waiting for, was it the end, or the beginning of something young and fresh? Oh would that that new, brighter life would come quickly, when it would be possible to look one's fate boldly in the face, know oneself to be right, and be happy and free! And such a life would come sooner or later' (*Betrothed*). In such passages the phrase 'in three or four hundred years' occurs with the regularity of a refrain, and Chekhov even used it, says Kuprin, in conversation. Dreaming of the future happiness of others, he 'was eagerly interested in new and original buildings, steamers, inventions, and was not bored by specialists. He said that crimes such as murder, theft and adultery were decreasing and believed that in the future true culture would ennoble mankind.' He shared, in his later years at least, the belief of his age in progress. 'The Russian intelligentsia loved Chekhov and Gorky,' says Merezhkovsky, 'because they taught them to believe in the triumph of progress, science, human reason, everything that is summed up in the phrase "humane ideas."' Chekhov himself wrote in 1902 to Dyagilev: 'Of the cultured classes of our society we may say that they have moved away from religion and will continue to move further and further away, whatever may be said about it, and whatever philosophico-religious societies may be founded. Whether this is a good thing or a bad thing I will not try to decide. I will only say that the religious movement of which you write is one thing, and the whole culture of to-day is another thing, which it will never be possible to bring under the former. Modern culture is the beginning of work for a great future, a work that will perhaps continue for tens of thousands of years in order that, even if only in the remote future, humanity may come to know the truth about the real God: not guess at it, that is, or look for it in Dostoevsky, but know it clearly, as it knows that twice two are four. Modern culture is the beginning of this work, but the religious movement in question is a survival, almost the last trace of something that has ceased or is ceasing to exist.' As if this were not explicit enough, he says in a later letter that he has long ceased to believe, and that any intelligent believer is a puzzle to him.

For all that, the sympathy and understanding with which Chekhov treats religious subjects is, as Chapter VI indicated, remarkable. There is none of the irony of an Anatole France in his pictures of the orthodox clergy, from village priests to bishops, and no one could be more sensitive to the beauty and impressiveness of the rites of the church. Particularly striking is his understanding of the monk who wrote songs of praise in *Easter Eve*, and of the bishop, so lonely as a man and so strong in the spirit through prayer and worship. No one would know that these things were not the work of a believer, and in view of his treatment of officials, for instance, one feels that he must have gone out of his way to avoid anything derogatory to the church, though by all accounts he would not have lacked material if he had chosen otherwise. The only explanation seems to be that though his intelligence made him doubt, his heart and imagination were still held captive by the traditional religion of his country.

The student, a favourite with Chekhov, reinforces this impression. We are told here how simple people in a remote village are moved to tears, on the eve of Good Friday, by a student's artless narration of what had happened nineteen centuries before on this same night in the High Priest's courtyard. 'The story he had just told,' the student thought, 'had some relationship to the present, to this desolate village, to himself, to all men. The past was linked to the present by an unbroken chain of events proceeding one from another. And it seemed to him that he had just seen both ends of the chain: he had touched one, and the other had stirred. The truth and beauty which had guided human life there in the high priest's yard had continued without interruption to this day, and had clearly always been the chief thing in human life and indeed in the whole world.' ⟨. . .⟩

[Chekov] looked back with longing to the days when he shared the common faith, and he was filled with that post-Christian nostalgia for faith so common since Romantic times, though like many others he often concealed his feelings under a mask of irony.

—W. H. Bruford, *Chekhov and His Russia: A Sociological Study* (New York: Oxford University Press, 1948): 208–210.

John Gassner on Chekhov's Cautious Optimism

[Distinguished American critic and scholar John Gassner (1903–1967) was Sterling Professor of Playwriting and Dramatic Literature at Yale University and was drama critic for *Educational Theater Journal* and other periodicals. He was also head of the Play Department of the Theater Guild in New York. His books include *Masters of the Drama and Form* and *Idea in Modern Theater*. In this passage, Gassner discusses Chekhov's cautious optimism and his conception of personal salvation.]

Characters with whom Chekhov is in obvious sympathy often carry Chekhov's favorite work theme, based upon the belief that salvation for the individual or at least balm for his suffering lies in creativity. Nina, in *The Seagull*, is going to make a good actress of herself even after the failure of her love-affair with the novelist Trigorin; and while Uta Hagen played the role in the attractive Theater Guild production of the 1930s, there could be no doubt that Nina would become one. "If only one could live the remnant of one's life in some new way," cries Uncle Vanya and adds, "we must make haste and work, make haste and do something." Irina, in *The Three Sisters*, cries out at the end, "I will give all my life to those to whom it may be of use," and her fiancé, the Baron, pathetically rejoices at the prospect of exchanging his aristocratic profession of arms for useful employment. "Something formidable is threatening us," he says. "The strong cleansing storm is gathering . . . it will soon sweep our world clean of laziness, indifference, prejudice against work, and wretched boredom." Regardless of Chekhov's dissatisfaction with the early Moscow Art Theater productions of his plays, Stanislavsky came to appreciate the fact that Chekhov's characters possessed a high degree of resilience. In *My Life in Art*, Stanislavsky denied that they were moribund: "Like Chekhov, [they] seek life, joy, laughter, courage . . . [they try] to overcome the hard and unbearable impasses into which life has plunged them."

Chekhov himself continued his exertions as long as his health permitted; he practiced medicine among the peasants and on one famous occasion took an arduous trip to the Siberian peninsula of Sakhalin for the purpose of investigating Russia's prison camps. Outstanding in his mind were the two necessities: social reform and the application of scientific knowledge to human suffering. "God's earth is good," he once wrote with characteristic simplicity after his travels. "It is only we on it who are bad. Instead of knowledge, there is insolence and boundless conceit; instead of labor, idleness and caddishness; there is no justice, the understanding of honor does not go beyond the honor of the uniform! . . .the important thing is that we must be just and all the rest will follow from this." He was equally plain-spoken on the subject of science. "Surgery alone," he once declared, "has accomplished so much that the very thought of it is frightening. The period of twenty years ago appears just pitiful to anyone studying medicine nowadays. . . . If I were presented the choice of one of the two, the 'ideals' of the sixties or the worst community hospital of the present time, I wouldn't hesitate a moment in choosing the latter." He reminds us in this respect of another great devotee of art whose roots lay in the nineteenth century—Ibsen's English champion and translator, William Archer—who expressed his gratitude for the scientists who discovered anesthetics, "balsam anodyne," who did more for man than religion did in reducing the amount of pain in the world. Chekhov spoke plainly on this subject when he wrote "I am not in the same camp with literary men who take a skeptical attitude toward science." ⟨. . .⟩

Chekhov the man and the writer, ⟨. . .⟩ belongs to the clear and broad, if by no means untroubled, stream of progressive modernism, to the modernism of hope rather than despair, and of activism rather than supine passiveness.

For Chekhov, who suffered from tuberculosis during half his lifetime and who died at the age of forty-four, the vivacity of health was not an easy possession. His health of spirit was hard-won and heroically maintained. Sympathy combined with skepticism helped him to maintain his balance under tension. He was a master of irony, and irony was in his case a sensible defense against excessive expectation on the part of one who believed in the possibility of progress. When his characters (such as Colonel Vershinin in *The Three Sisters*) spout optimism unbounded, it is plain that they are *troubled*. They do not speak the sentiments of their author, who remains more or less ironically aloof, although by no means hostile or indifferent toward them. It is plain that he did not share their protestations of deferred hope without a substantial discount.

Chekhov, to sum up, transcended the superficiality that often adheres to optimistic literature and at the same time escaped the morbidity that besets pessimistic profundity; and he kept a characteristic balance in other important respects. He stood virtually alone among the modern literary masters after 1890 in being complex without some mystique and subtle without obscurity. He was, so to speak, Olympian and yet also thoroughly companionable. It is chiefly by bearing these polarities in mind, and remembering especially the plain yet somehow elusive fact that there was ever sympathy in his comedy and some degree of comedy in his sympathy, that we may hope to bring his plays authentically to the stage.

> —John Gassner, "The Duality of Chekhov." In *Chekhov: A Collection of Critical Essays*, edited by Robert Louis Jackson (Englewood Cliffs, NJ: Prentice-Hall, 1967): 181–183.

SIEGFRIED MELCHINGER ON THE SYMBOLISM OF MOSCOW

[Siegfried Melchinger has written *The Concise Encyclopaedia of Modern Drama* as well as books on the works of Sophocles and Euripides. In this passage on *The Three Sisters*, Melchinger writes about the sisters' desperate yearning for Moscow and what Moscow symbolizes.]

And what is this Moscow, on which the sisters put all their hopes? It is a real memory, but heavily embroidered and eventually exposed as an illusion. Eleven years ago they had to leave the scene of their happy childhood, because their father was assigned to a provincial garrison. At the time Olga was seventeen, Masha perhaps thirteen, and Irina a little girl of nine. In the dreary reality of the provincial town, Moscow has become more and more the golden city of their dreams. In the first act they are still quite sure that now that the year of mourning is over, they will soon move back to Moscow. Besides, their brother will surely get a professorship there. What a happy omen they see in the fact that Vershinin, the new colonel, who makes a courtesy call on them, not only comes from Moscow but had even been a visitor to the general's house there (he then was called "the lovesick major"). The dream's golden glow transfigures this man who is now in his early forties and who brings a new note into the usual conversations. A philosopher, he gives the sisters the most beautiful compliments. In the future, he says, in two or three hundred years hence, everything will be different. A happier time will dawn, and "if then, in a desolate, dreary town like this one, there are three human beings like you," that would be proof enough that things are slowly turning for the better. The colonel goes on to say:

> "Of course, you cannot conquer the dull mass around you, and in the course of your lives you will have to forsake, bit by bit, parts of yourselves. Life will smother you. And yet, you shall not simply fade away, without leaving a trace of light behind you. After you, there will perhaps be six, and then twelve people like yourselves, and so on, until finally human beings of your kind will be in the majority. In two or three hundred years, life on earth will be unimaginably beautiful and grand."

Now, that these trivial ideas are expressed for the first time, the girls hear in them only the note of hope, and the man who says them makes them happy with these words. But in the next act Chekhov has the colonel return repeatedly to this idea. His only conversational topic is this "philosophy," which he trots out at any opportunity—an ironic variation on the play's basic theme. Its contradiction, which others, with opposing arguments, set against it—"life will always stay as it is now, and in two hundred years hence people will sigh as they do now and say, 'How hard life is!'"—is another ironic variation of the same theme. The illusory quality of these conceptions resemble the illusory character of the sisters' Moscow dream, which drives them, as one of them says, "nearly mad." They simply don't listen when the colonel tries to talk them out of their Moscow idea: "People won't even notice that you're there." Moscow is a city like others, life there is just as it is everywhere else; the city of your dream is merely a phantom. By the third act no one listens any longer when the colonel expounds his philosophy. "I think they have all gone to sleep," he observes. And when he starts in on it even while making his farewell, he admits, "I have talked too much—please don't hold it against me!" Subdued, he adds to his chatter about life in two hundred years' time: "If it only would happen sooner!"

—Siegfried Melchinger, *Anton Chekhov,* translated by Edith Tarcov (New York: Frederick Ungar Publishing, 1972): 139–140.

Karl D. Kramer on Andrey and Chebutykin

[Karl D. Kramer is associate professor of Slavic languages and literatures and comparative literature at the University of Washington. He is the author of works on Chekhov, impressionism, and Garshin. In this essay on *The Three Sisters*, Kramer focuses on the characters of Andrey and Chebutykin.]

It is Andrey's fate to make the most ghastly miscalculation of them all in believing he loves Natasha. How could he, an educated man, brought up in the same environment as his sisters, believe he has fallen in love with her? Masha in the first act discounts the possibility that he could be serious about her. The answer seems to lie in a recognition that he has been constantly living under pressures he can't bear. "Father . . . oppressed us with education. . . . I grew fat in one year after he died, as if my body were liberated from his oppression," he tells Vershinin. He has been preparing for a university career, bowing to his father's wishes—a course he abandons immediately after his marriage. Since the father's death, Andrey has been under constant pressure from his sisters to deliver them from this provincial town. His love for Natasha is simply a means of escaping these various responsibilities, which have been thrust upon him. But a relationship based on such motivation becomes a trap from which Andrey desperately wishes to escape. In some dialogue that Chekhov eventually deleted from the play, Andrey dreams of losing all his money, being deserted by his wife, running back to his sisters, crying, "I'm saved! I'm saved!" In the finished play, Andrey and Chebutykin argue about the efficacy of marriage, Andrey maintaining it is to be avoided, Chebutykin asserting loneliness is worse. But by the end of the play, even Chebutykin admits that the best course for Andrey is to leave, "leave and keep going, don't ever look back." This is, indeed, the course Chebutykin himself adopts at the end of the play. Andrey's escape from responsibility through love thus seems to lead only to an entrapment from which he would be only too happy to flee by the end of the play. His predicament stems not so much from Natasha's nature as from his own desire to avoid experience by hiding behind a very illusory kind of love.

Chebutykin's problems turn equally on love. He had at one time known a real love for the sisters' mother. That has long been in the past, but the only vaguely positive way he can deal with immediate experience is by the illusion that this love can be sustained through his relationship with the sisters, particularly Irina. His other protective screen is his growing insistence that nothing and nobody really exists and that therefore nothing matters. In his first appearance at stage center, he is talking sheer nonsense about a remedy for baldness and duly noting down this trivia. Shortly thereafter in Act I he displays his tender—almost sentimental—affection for Irina by presenting her with a silver samovar on her name day. The fact that the silver samovar is the traditional gift on the twenty-fifth wedding anniversary surely suggests that he is honoring the memory of the woman he loved and is exploiting the occasion of Irina's name day for this purpose. During the first two acts he alternates between these two poles—the attempt to sustain a lost love and an abiding interest in trivia. The chief sign of the latter is his constant reading of old newspapers, a device for distracting himself from the actuality of the present moment.

In Act III his failure to handle his experience reaches a crisis when, drunk, realizing he is responsible for the death of a woman who was under his care, he retreats into a pretense that nothing and nobody exists. It may be a measure of his feeling that he so retreats, but I would suggest that he associates this recent death with that death in the past of the woman he loved. Death has denied him his love, and the recent event vividly reminds him of his own earlier loss. Within moments of this breakdown he smashes the clock which had belonged to the sisters' mother. This may of course suggest that he is trying to destroy time itself, which separates him from his love, but he is also deliberately destroying a material object that belonged to her; it may also be a gesture of denial—a denial that his love ever existed. He tries to cover this by suggesting that perhaps there was no clock to break, and he accuses the others of refusing to see that Natasha and Protopopov are having an affair. The assumption is that if others don't see what's right before their eyes, why shouldn't Chebutykin refuse to recognize anything in the world that may hurt him? In any case, what comes out of this episode is our discovery that Chebutykin cannot deal with a death that takes away his love. His final stance in the play—"The baron is a fine fellow, but one baron more or less, what difference does it make?" (XI, 294)—is a pathetic indication of the lengths he is driven to in trying to cope with a love long since lost.

> —Karl Kramer, "*Three Sisters*, or Taking a Chance on Love." In *Chekhov's Great Plays: A Critical Anthology*, edited by Jean-Pierre Barricelli (New York: New York University Press, 1981): 62–64.

EUGENE BRISTOW ON THE STAGING OF *THE THREE SISTERS*

[Eugene Bristow is professor in the department of Theater and Drama at the Russian and East European Institute, Indiana University at Bloomington. He has written works on Ostrovskiy, Chekhov, Blok, Meyerkhol'd, variety theater, and directing for the stage. In this passage, Bristow discusses the staging of *The Three Sisters* and the grouping of characters within the play.]

The effect of Chekhov's opening and closing in *The Three Sisters* is similar to that of the chorus in ancient Greek tragedy; that is, two groups, separated in space, sing and dance their choral odes; the first is called a strophe; the second, antistrophe. At the beginning, the answering group upstage consists of three military officers, Tuzenbakh, Solenyy, and Chebutykin, who are talking together. What is heard by the audience, however, is an ironic comment on what the downstage group (the sisters Ol'ga, Masha, and Irina) is doing and saying. That Chekhov deliberately arranged this opening in terms of the Greek chorus is verified by a comparison of the Yalta manuscript (an early version) with the Moscow manuscript (a late version). The three verbal combinations of the upstage group have been added, including Tuzenbakh's apparent comment to Solenyy (in reality, a summary conclusion on the optimistic dreams of the sisters): "You're talking so much nonsense I'm sick of listening to you." It should be noted that not one character in either group is aware of the chorus device. The aspirations expressed in the downstage odes are consistently denied by the negative comments in the upstage odes. The result is an appropriate stalemate in which the downstage three sisters are perfectly balanced by the upstage three military officers.

The grouping of characters in threes occurs throughout; moreover, membership in one group does not exclude membership in another, since both members and groups are constantly in flux. The Prozorov family is a good example.

Ol'ga

Irina   Masha

Andrey

The family quartet is viewed as a foursome only for a few moments in the first act, when Andrey is called in to meet Vershinin and for a single moment in the third act, just before Masha leaves to meet Vershinin. Combinations of these four Prozorovs into threesomes, however, take place on six or perhaps seven occasions. For example, in addition to the opening and close, the sisters share important scenes with Vershinin in Act I and Natasha in Act IV and develop one of their own in Act III. Andrey, Masha, and Irina are together for the party in Act II, and Ol'ga and Irina behind their screens apparently listen to Andrey's confession near the end of Act III. It might be argued that this last scene—the seventh—is not really a threesome, since Andrey is the only visible character onstage, and neither sister acknowledges his presence or his words once they have escaped behind the screens.

The concept of three pervades the stories, particularly the love stories, in the play. Love triangles, with varying combinations, complicate the action, adding interest and suspense. Three triangles are apparently the most important. Baron Tuzenbakh loves Irina, as does Solenyy who tells Irina his feelings in Act II.

Irina, however, does not love either one, but is persuaded by Ol'ga in Act III to become the fiancée of Tuzenbakh. In the first act, Kulygin loves his wife Masha, who, in turn, is falling in love with Lieutenant Colonel Vershinin. Vershinin declares his love in Act II, and in the following act, Masha tells her sisters that she has fallen in love with Vershinin. Masha does not love her husband, nor does Vershinin love his wife. At the end of Act I, Andrey declares his love to Natasha, and between Acts I and II they marry and Natasha births a son, whom she calls Bobik. Her affair with Protopopov is discussed later in this essay. Andrey, who is very much aware of Natasha's adultery, inexplicably still loves her, as he tells the doctor in Act IV.

  —Eugene K. Bristow, "Circles, Triads, and Parity in *The Three Sisters*." In *Chekhov's Great Plays: A Critical Anthology*, edited by Jean-Pierre Barricelli (New York: New York University Press, 1981): 77–79.

Maurice Valency on Chekhov and the Combination of Comedy and Tragedy

[Maurice Valency is Professor Emeritus of Dramatic Literature, Columbia University, and Director of Academic Studies at the Julliard School. He is the author of works on Chekhov, Ibsen, Strindberg, Shaw, and medieval literature. He is also a playwright and librettist. In this essay on *The Three Sisters*, Valency discusses Chekhov's technique of weaving comedy together with tragedy to achieve something new.]

With *The Three Sisters* Chekhov in some sense initiated a genre in the drama, and one can readily sympathize with the dismay of the company of actors that first heard it read. Plays with stock characters and a strong, clear anecdote are easiest to play. *The Three Sisters* is relatively plotless. It interweaves four narrative themes so as to form a texture, but it has none of the usual amenities of the *pièce bien faite*. The action is molded into something like unity by means of the theme of waste and the enclosing symbol of the unattainable city. What is achieved in this manner hardly leaps to the eye. *The Three Sisters* is, at bottom, a novel.

For the rest, the portraiture is executed with the broad, epigrammatic strokes of the impressionist, so that much is left to the imagination. In a novel such techniques may be considered advantageous, since when the degree of control is minimal, the reader is at liberty to exercise his wits, with a consequent intensification of the work's vitality. On the stage the problem becomes embarrassing. A production necessarily involves an interpretation and is, in some measure, exclusive. The actor who plays Vershinin, for example, will be convincing only insofar as he realizes the character he is meant to portray, and the manner in which the other characters react to his portrayal will, to a great extent, determine the mood and meaning of the play. In *The Three Sisters*, Andrey, Solenyy, Chebutykin, and Tuzenbakh are relatively clear characters, and none of the young ladies offers any unusual difficulty of interpretation. But the play provides little guidance for the interpretation of Vershinin.

In such circumstances Stanislavskiy was accustomed to ask his actors to rummage their souls. But it is a rare actor who can manage to locate a Vershinin in his soul. Normally what the actor finds there is some equivalent aspect of himself or, more likely, some reflection of the director's self, depending on whose is the more dominant personality; and there is no reason to assume that either version will represent to the audience the universal Vershinin, much less the particular Vershinin who took shape in the author's mind when he composed his play. In consequence, Vershinin is normally played as a stereotype, and the actor is usually offered a choice of several. Those who consider, as did Stanislavskiy, that Chekhov was at bottom a tragic writer, tend to make Vershinin a pathetic figure, the manly, but submissive victim of his *moira*, perhaps, in some sense, the military counterpart of Trigorin. Those who insist that Chekhov's bent was predominantly ironic and satirical see Vershinin as a wistful comedian, like Gayev, a futile figure whose philosophical tirades are habitually received with impatient snickers, or with boredom. Finally, those of a Marxist turn of mind are likely to dignify Vershinin as a precursor of the Russian Revolution, a prophet of the future who is sick with the illness of the times, and is thus unable to lift a finger to bring about the wonders he foresees. To this list of possibilities there must certainly be added the posture of the cautious professional who moves warily though his lines without committing himself in any way, careful to offend no one with a definite intonation or gesture.

The responsibility for this confusion must be laid, once again, at Chekhov's door. Unwilling, apparently, to engage himself completely with regard to *The Three Sisters*, a play that had already caused him much trouble, he left his actors, in the words of Vladimir Yermilov, to "cudgel their brains over the question: is it a comedy or a tragedy? not knowing whether to laugh or to cry...." This critic continues:

> Chekhov worked out an aesthetic principle according to which the tragic and the comic are divided by no wall, but merely represent the two sides of one and the same phenomenon of life, which has its tragic and its comic sides. Any phenomenon, from Chekhov's point of view, can be regarded simultaneously in a tragic and a comic aspect.

—Maurice Valency, "Vershinin." In *Chekhov's Great Plays: A Critical Anthology*, edited by Jean-Pierre Barricelli (New York: New York University Press, 1981): 221–223.

Plot Summary of
The Cherry Orchard

The Cherry Orchard is about the demise of a way of life, of a whole social class in Russia, but Chekhov is careful to neither strictly glorify or demonize this change. Unable to tolerate didacticism in art, he both exalts and laments the passing of the land-owning gentility. The orchard in the play is a famous one, having had a long and illustrious life in the Ranevskaya family, but the crucial moment has come: the family is bankrupt and they must decide the fate of the estate, and thus their own future. Lyubov, her two daughters, Anya and Varya, and her brother Gaev must try to find a way to prevent the authorities from auctioning off their estate in order to pay their debts. But Lyubov and Gaev stridently ignore the problem, against all warnings, letting the problem take care of itself. Chekhov draws characters so consumed by fear of reality and so willing to evade the truth that they are absurd; thus the play is subtitled "A Comedy."

Lopakhin is the antagonist in the play, if such a label can be applied to any Chekhov character. Although Lopakhin tries repeatedly to help the Ranevskayas out of their predicament, in the end he devours them. Lopakhin is from a family of serfs who formerly worked on the orchard. He has grown rich as a merchant and offers a practical scenario to save the Ranevskayas if not the orchard itself. He proposes that they chop down the trees, divide the land into small plots, and sell them to the increasing population of holiday makers. This would increase the family fortune immensely, though it would not preserve the orchard itself, but the Ranevskayas cannot consent to the destruction of their beloved orchard. They make a poor effort to come up with another plan, however, and in the end, the estate is auctioned, Lopakhin becomes the owner, and the trees are felled before their very eyes.

The defining moment of the play, the scene most filled with a frenzied pathos and lunacy, is the ball held at the estate while its fate is being decided at an auction in town. The party, orchestrated by Lyubov, is a dance of death, a last desperate attempt to breathe life into what is dying. This is an extreme example of Chekhov's unique approach to plot—while the essential action is happening off-stage, something seemingly totally unrelated is happening on-stage. But the truth is lurking ominously in the background, and no one, in the play or in the audience, is unaware.

In **Act One**, Lopakhin and Dunyasha sit in the Ranevskaya home awaiting the arrival of Lyubov, the family matriarch, who has been living abroad for five years. Lyubov is an generous, extravagant woman, unable—or more likely, unwilling—to be practical. The orchard was her inheritance from her father, but she married a penniless drunk who died some years ago. She quickly fell in love again and went abroad with her lover, but soon after she took leave, her little boy Grisha drowned in the nearby river. The orchard has become even more precious to her as a result. It is the place she spent her blissful youth and the place where her son met his end. After Lyubov nurses her lover through a grave illness, however, he stole her remaining money and left. She tried to commit suicide and failed. Having lost everything, including hope, she returns to the orchard.

Lyubov, her daughter Anya, and Anya's governess Sharlotta arrive, momentarily elated at the site of their beautiful orchard. Varya, Lyubov's adopted daughter, greets them happily, but announces soon, however, that the estate will be auctioned in August. Varya is hopeful that Anya will marry someone rich and they will be saved. She is practical and devout. She wishes to go to a cloister when everything has been resolved. But she is not heard, and Gaev, Lyubov's brother, interjects an imaginary game of billiards that he plays aloud intermittently throughout the play. "An English shot into the corner!" is hardly an appropriate response to impending doom. It highlights the distance he and his family maintain from reality.

Lopakhin, who harbors a secret love for Lyubov, offers his plan to save the orchard and Lyubov responds, "I don't quite understand you." Lopakhin points out that the orchard can no longer support itself. There is only one crop every two years and the market is now flooded with cherries. <u>Their orchard is no longer needed; it is merely beautiful. The orchard becomes a symbol for the Ranevskayas themselves.</u>

Gaev's unenthusiastic attempt at saving the orchard is to send Anya to see her grandmother, a countess, to ask for funds. Gaev gives his word of honor that the estate will not be sold, but his kind of honor is now useless.

The inability of the Ranevskayas to act can be interpreted either as impotence or as an acceptance of the inevitable. They know that to destroy their own orchard and sell it off to the bourgeois for cash will be equivalent to becoming one of them, becoming Lopakhin. Since this is intolerable, their only task now is to die with dignity.

Act Two is set outside, where telegraph poles are visible in the distance, marring the beautiful landscape. The various servants of the estate sit together and make comic banter. Yepikhodov is in love with Dunyasha, who is in love with Yasha. Yepikhodov speaks despairingly about his life, but he projects only small-minded self-satisfaction.

> I can't comprehend at all the directions I personally want to take that is, to go on living or to shoot myself, personally speaking. But nonetheless I always carry a revolver on me. Here it is . . .

Sharlotta, the governess, rounds out the picture as she sits, eating a cucumber, lamenting that she has no one.

Lyubov, Gaev, and Lopakhin join them. While Lopakhin makes his second attempt to convince them of the necessity of an immediate decision, Lyubov hears music in the distance and wonders who is playing. When her brother tells her it is the Jewish orchestra, she proposes to send for them some time and have a party. Lyubov proposes that Lopakhin marry Varya, not out of cunning, but because Varya has expressed genuine interest in Lopakhin. But even though Lopakhin will be presented with ample opportunity, and will even lead her on, he will never ask her. He shows himself to be somewhat cruel in this.

Firs, Gaev's old manservant, joins the conversation, and he, as much as the Ranevskayas themselves, bemoans the future and glorifies the past. The old order helped him understand his place in life. The new order is frightening and chaotic.

> I've been living a long time now . . . When freedom came for the serfs, I was already the head valet. I did not accept freedom at that time, so I kept on with the master and mistress . . . Oh, I remember everyone was glad, but what they were glad about, why, they didn't even know themselves.

Though he is from the peasantry, Firs is equally ill-suited for the new world where men like Lopakhin are the winners.

Lopakhin is a new breed. He is a hard worker, with a shrewd business sense, a willingness to take risks and to put money before even friendship. He is not without any virtue, as he honorably tries to save the Ranevskayas, but he is without sensitivity or culture. Lopakhin admits that he can barely read.

Lopakhin's opposite is not the Ranevskayas, with whom he does have some sympathy, some admiration. Instead, Trofimov is Lopakhin's antithesis. Trofimov is the teacher who has also become part of the orchard's landscape. He was once tutor to little Grisha, who drowned in the river, and he has lived on the estate since. He is a perpetual student who loves to make declarations, living in his idealistic future where everyone will work. Ironically, Lopakhin and Trofimov are both proponents of work, Lopakhin being the realization while Trofimov merely talks. But Lopakhin and Trofimov do not understand one another at all.

Chekhov's concept of the overwrought academic, such as Trofimov, is someone ridiculous. Chekhov did not admire academia, which he felt to be too often idle and self-important. Trofimov does not realize that he is pointing to himself when he says, "We must stop admiring ourselves. What we ought to do is just keep working." He declares that he is "above love" and that his strong feelings for Anya are more than mere love. Lyubov, in spite of her thoughtlessness, understands Trofimov and finds him to be endearingly absurd. She knows the truth about him. She calls him "an immaculate prude . . . a laughable eccentric boy, some kind of freak . . ." Trofimov foretells the ending of the old order and convinces Anya that redemption can only come when the orchard is destroyed.

> . . . we must first of all redeem our past and then be done with it forever. And the only way we can redeem our past is by suffering and by giving ourselves over to exceptional labor, to steadfast and endless work. You must realize this, Anya.

As this group sits together they hear, for the first time, the sound of a breaking string far off in the distance. Chekhov never clearly defines this mysterious sound, but apparently it is a metaphoric collapse. It is the whole universe straining toward something that finally snaps; if nothing else, it is an ending. The breaking string will surface again at the very end of the play.

Act Three is the party Lyubov mentioned earlier, attended by the Jewish orchestra. It is a ludicrous expense, while off in town, the estate is auctioned and all is lost. Everyone is present except Gaev and Lopakhin, who are in town at the auction. Whatever we may have felt toward Lyubov and her penchant for daydreams, we feel real empathy for her when, while everyone is pathetically rejoicing around her, she says:

> Without the cherry orchard my life would lose its meaning and if it must really be sold then go and sell me with the orchard . . . You see my son was drowned here . . . Have pity on me, my fine, kind friend.

Gaev returns finally from town with Lopakhin and the announcement is made that the estate has been sold and now belongs to Lopakhin. Lopakhin gleefully plans the destruction of the orchard, right there in front of the Ranevskayas.

Act Four is a departure. Furniture is piled in a corner and suitcases are waiting to be taken to the train. Even so, Yasha serves champagne. Lopakhin callously, though not viciously, tells everyone he plans to plant acres of poppies. Gaev decides to take a job at the bank. Trofimov is going to Moscow to the university. Anya tries to comfort her mother with visions of a new and better life, and Lyubov does not try to injure her daughter's unrealistic dreams. Anya plans to become a teacher, while Lyubov is leaving for Paris. Varya has agreed to become a housekeeper. Lyubov and Gaev have a silent tender moment alone as they weep in each other's arms. Everyone exits and only Firs, the old servant, is left on stage.

Firs is ill. He was supposed to have been taken to the hospital, but he was lost in the shuffle and remains on-stage alone, lying down feebly. He wonders aloud if Gaev has his fur coat.

> I just didn't look after it . . . Oh, these green young things—they never learn! . . . Life just slipped by as if I'd never even lived . . . I'll lie down for while . . . You just don't have any strength, none, nothing's left, nothing at all . . . Oh you . . . silly galoot, you!

These are the play's last words, spoken fittingly by Firs, who will die very soon, like his way of life. In the background is the sound of an axe striking a tree and the sound of string breaking. ❧

List of Characters in
The Cherry Orchard

Lyubov Andreevna Ranevskaya, a landowner, is the matriarch of the family. She has been abroad for five years when the play opens, and she is just returning to find out that her beloved orchard is going to be sold. The family is bankrupt, and no one can come up with a reasonable solution to save the estate. She is thoughtless and extravagant but lovable and generous, a dignified member of the gentry.

Anya, her daughter, is an idealistic 17-year-old girl, in love with Trofimov and eager to start a new life away from the orchard. She was sent to Paris to retrieve her despairing mother and returns with her at the opening of the play.

Varya, her adopted daughter, age 24, is a pious and pragmatic young woman, who has hopes for saving the orchard, but she also has alternate plans. She imagines herself living in a convent, although she does have an attachment to Lopakhin, who expresses some interest in her as well. He will never propose, however, and she will end up as a housekeeper on another estate.

Leonid Andreevich Gaev, brother of Lyubov Ranevskaya, is a feckless but genteel man, who, like his sister, refuses to confront the impending sale of the orchard until it is too late. He is perpetually playing an imaginary game of billiards, while coming up with a multitude of improbable schemes for securing enough money to save them.

Yermolay Alexeevich Lopakhin, a merchant, is the son of serfs who once worked and lived on the orchard. He has become very wealthy as a businessman and tries to offer the Ranevskayas a way out of their debt. When they don't listen, however, he buys the estate himself and begins hacking away at the trees before they have even left the estate. Lopakhin means well, but he is base and opportunistic and does not understand the delicate natures of the Ranevskayas, nor the monumental significance of the passing of the orchard.

Pyotr Sergeevich Trofimov, a student, was once tutor to Lyubov's now deceased son. He has managed to stay on the estate since the death five years previous. He has fallen in love with Anya, and in his idealistic reverie, he imagines that he is "above love." He is an advocate of work, and he does not mourn the death of the orchard, even though he has become part of it himself.

Boris Borisovich Simeonov-Pishchik, a landowner, is a clownish figure who quotes Nietzsche to justify forging bank notes. He is himself in a precarious situation with regards to his land. He owes and cannot come up with the money, but unlike the Ranevskayas, he thinks constantly about money. He professes to have fallen in love with Sharlotta.

Sharlotta Ivanovna, a governess, accompanied Anya to Paris and returns with them. She is famous for her tricks, which she performs at every given opportunity, even while the final verdict of the orchard is being read.

Semyon Panteleevich Yepikhodov, a clerk, pursues Dunyasha, but Dunyasha is not interested in him. He laments his fate in a comical manner, always carrying a revolver around should he decide to shoot himself. He claims he is tossed around by fate.

Dunyasha, a maidservant, is a ridiculous woman who throws herself at Yasha without inhibition. But Yasha is not in love with her, though he does tease her.

Firs, an old manservant, age eighty-seven, is a relic of the past. He is devoted to his masters, who treat him well. He is perpetually following Gaev around inquiring about his needs. Firs is a gentle, simple man, who was happier when there was a more distinct social order, when he felt he understood his place.

Yasha, a young manservant, begs Lyubov to take him with her to Paris. He wants escape. He is a social climber who will become engaged to Dunyasha but not seriously and not publicly. ❈

Critical Views on
The Cherry Orchard

MAXIM GORKY ON CHEKHOV'S TRAGIC HUMOR

[Maxim Gorky (1868–1936), a friend and colleague of Chekhov's, was a Russian novelist, short-story writer, and playwright. He was imprisoned several times for his Marxist writings and for his participation in the Revolution of 1905. After the Revolution, Gorky was able to intercede and often save the lives of many literary figures. Among his works are: *Mother*, his autobiographical trilogy *Childhood, In the World*, and *My Universities, Notes from a Diary, The Artamonov Business* and various plays. In this essay, Gorky discusses Chekhov's tragic humor, especially his comedic conception of banality.]

When a man is young, banality seems only amusing and unimportant, but little by little it possesses a man; it permeates his brain and blood like a poison or asphyxiating fumes; he becomes like an old, rusty signboard: something is painted on it, but what?—You can't make out.

Anton Pavlovich in his early stories was already able to reveal in the dim sea of banality its tragic humour; one has only to read his "humorous" stories with attention to see what a lot of cruel and disgusting things, behind the humorous words and situations, had been observed by the author with sorrow and were concealed by him.

He was ingenuously shy; he would not say aloud and openly to people: "Now do be more decent"; he hoped in vain that they would themselves see how necessary it was that they should be more decent. He hated everything banal and foul, and he described the abominations of life in the noble language of a poet, with the humorist's gentle smile, and behind the beautiful form of his stories people scarcely noticed the inner meaning, full of bitter reproach.

The dear public, when it reads his *Daughter of Albion*, laughs and hardly realizes how abominable is the well-fed squire's mockery of a person who is lonely and strange to everyone and everything. In each of his humorous stories I hear the quiet, deep sigh of a pure and human heart, the hopeless sigh of sympathy for men who do not know how to respect human dignity, who submit without any resistance to mere force, live like fish, believe in nothing but the necessity of swallowing every day as much thick soup as possible, and feel nothing but fear that someone, strong and insolent, will give them a hiding.

No one understood as clearly and finely as Anton Chekhov the tragedy of life's trivialities, no one before him showed men with such merciless truth the terrible and shameful picture of their life in the dim chaos of bourgeois everyday existence.

His enemy was banality; he fought it all his life long; he ridiculed it, drawing it with a pointed and unimpassioned pen, finding the mustiness of banality even where at the first glance everything seemed to be arranged very nicely, comfortably, and even brilliantly—and banality revenged itself upon him by a nasty prank, for it saw that his corpse, the corpse of a poet, was put into a railway truck "For the Conveyance of Oysters."

That dirty green railway truck seems to me precisely the great, triumphant laugh of banality over its tired enemy; and all the "Recollections" in the gutter Press are hypocritical sorrow, behind which I feel the cold and smelly breath of banality, secretly rejoicing over the death of its enemy.

~

Reading Anton Chekhov's stories, one feels oneself in a melancholy day of late autumn, when the air is transparent and the outline of naked trees, narrow houses, greyish people, is sharp. Everything is strange, lonely, motionless, helpless. The horizon, blue and empty, melts into the pale sky, and its breath is terribly cold upon the earth, which is covered with frozen mud. The author's mind, like the autumn sun, shows up in hard outline the monotonous roads, the crooked streets, the little squalid houses in which tiny, miserable people are stifled by boredom and laziness and fill the houses with an unintelligible, drowsy bustle. Here, anxiously, like a grey mouse, scurries *The Darling*, the dear, meek woman who loves so slavishly and who can love so much. You can slap her cheek and she won't even dare to utter a sigh aloud, the meek slave. . . . And by her side is Olga of *The Three*

Sisters: she too loves much, and submits with resignation to the caprices of the dissolute, banal wife of her good-for-nothing brother; the life of her sisters crumbles before her eyes, she weeps and cannot help anyone in anything, and she has not within her a single live, strong word of protest against banality.

And here is the lachrymose Ranevskaya and the other owners of "The Cherry Orchard," egotistical like children, with the flabbiness of senility. They missed the right moment for dying; they whine, seeing nothing of what is going on around them, understanding nothing, parasites without the power of again taking root in life. The wretched little student, Trofimov, speaks eloquently of the necessity of working—and does nothing but amuse himself, out of sheer boredom, with stupid mockery of Varya, who works ceaselessly for the good of idlers.

Vershinin dreams of how pleasant life will be in three hundred years, and lives without perceiving that everything around him is falling into ruin before his eyes; Solyony, from boredom and stupidity, is ready to kill the pitiable Baron Tusenbach.

There passes before one a long file of men and women, slaves of their love, of their stupidity and idleness, of their greed for the good things of life; there walk the slaves of the dark fear of life; they struggle anxiously along, filling life with incoherent words about the future, feeling that in the present there is no place for them.

—Maxim Gorky, *Reminiscences of Tolstoy, Chekhov and Andreev*, translated by Katherine Mansfield, S. S. Koteliansky, and Leonard Woolf (London: The Hogarth Press, 1948): 107–111.

Francis Fergusson on the Suffering of Change in *The Cherry Orchard*

[Francis Fergusson is professor of comparative literature at Princeton University. He has published numerous critical studies, including *The Idea of Theater: A Study of Ten Plays* and other works on Dante, Chekhov, Greek plays, dramatic literature, and poetry. In this selection, Fergusson discusses *The Cherry Orchard* as a poem of the suffering of change.]

The family that owns the old estate named after its famous orchard—Lyubov, her brother Gaev, and her daughters Varya and Anya—is all but bankrupt, and the question is how to prevent the bailiffs from selling the estate to pay their debts. Lopahin, whose family were formerly serfs on the estate, is now rapidly growing rich as a businessman, and he offers a very sensible plan: chop down the orchard, divide the property into small lots, and sell them off to make a residential suburb for the growing industrial town nearby. Thus the cash value of the estate could be not only preserved, but increased. But this would not save what Lyubov and her brother find valuable in the old estate; they cannot consent to the destruction of the orchard. But they cannot find, or earn, or borrow the money to pay their debts either; and in due course the estate is sold at auction to Lopahin himself, who will make a very good thing of it. His workmen are hacking at the old trees before the family is out of the house.

The play may be briefly described as a realistic ensemble pathos: the characters all suffer the passing of the estate in different ways, thus adumbrating this change at a deeper and more generally significant level than that of any individual's experience. The action which they all share by analogy, and which informs the suffering of the destined change of the Cherry Orchard, is "to save the Cherry Orchard": that is, each character sees some value in it—economic, sentimental, social, cultural—which he wishes to keep. By means of his plot, Chekhov always focuses attention on the general action: his crowded stage, full of the characters I have mentioned as well as half a dozen hangers-on, is like an implicit discussion of the fatality which concerns them all; but Chekhov does not believe in their ideas, and the inter-play he shows among his *dramatis personae* is not so much the play of thought as the alternation of his characters' perceptions of their situation, as the moods shift and the time for decision comes and goes.

Though the action which Chekhov chooses to show on-stage is "pathetic," i.e., suffering and perception, it is complete: the Cherry Orchard is constituted before our eyes, and then dissolved. The first act is a prologue: it is the occasion of Lyubov's return from Paris to try to resume her old life. Through her eyes and those of her daughter Anya, as well as from the complementary perspectives of Lopahin and Trofimov, we see the estate as it were in the round, in its many possible meanings. The second act corresponds to the agon; it is in this act that we become aware of the conflicting values of all the characters, and of the efforts they make (offstage) to save each one *his* Orchard. The third act corresponds to the pathos and peripety of the traditional tragic form. The occasion is a rather hysterical party which Lyubov gives while her estate is being sold at auction in the nearby town; it ends with Lopahin's announcement, in pride and the bitterness of guilt, that he was the purchaser. The last act is the epiphany: we see the action, now completed, in a new and ironic light. The occasion is the departure of the family: the windows are boarded up, the furniture piled in the corners, and the bags packed. All the characters feel, and the audience sees in a thousand ways, that the wish to save the Orchard has amounted in fact to destroying it; the gathering of its denizens to separation; the homecoming to departure. What this "means" we are not told. But the action is completed, and the poem of the suffering of change concludes in a new and final perception, and a rich chord of feeling.

—Francis Fergusson, *The Idea of Theater: A Study of Ten Plays* (Princeton, N.J.: Princeton University Press, 1949): 162–164.

ILYA EHRENBURG ON THE SHADINGS OF CHARACTER IN CHEKHOV'S WORKS

[Ilya Ehrenburg (1891–1967) was a Soviet journalist, novelist, and political consort. He dined with Lenin, Trotsky, Stalin, and Krushchev. In this passage, Ehrenburg discusses Chekhov's subtle shadings of character which he employed over black and white depictions.]

In Chekhov's works you will not find pure white or pure black; this has sometimes been explained by the nature of the period, which was dull and grey. I believe that it would be more correct to speak of the nature of the artist. In those of his works devoted not to faded Liberals or muddle-headed intellectuals, but to art or love, we find an equally careful blending of colours, an equal wealth of nuances. The word 'realism' in itself will define nothing: Saltykov-Shchedrin in his satirical sketches, Gorky in his romantic early stories were also realists. It is more correct to say that in his striving to reveal the inner world of man, Chekhov did not use the methods of a graphic artist but those of a painter. His understanding of his task as a writer is best expressed in his comments on books by his predecessors. He thought highly of Turgenev but what he liked in his work was not what was then regarded as an almost obligatory matter for love and admiration. Here is what he said about Turgenev's women: '. . . all Turgenev's women and girls are insufferable because they are so contrived and, forgive me, false. Liza, Elena—those are not Russian girls but sort of Delphic oracles voicing mysterious pronouncements, full of pretensions unsuited to their station.' I have mentioned Chekhov's admiration for Tolstoy. Yet there were pages in his favourite novel which distressed him: 'Every night I wake up and read *War and Peace*. One reads it with as much curiosity and naïve surprise as though one had never read it before. It is wonderfully good. The only parts I don't like are those where Napoleon appears. As soon as Napoleon comes on the scene there is strain, and every kind of trick is used to prove that he was more stupid than he really was. Everything Pierre, Prince Andrey or that utter nonentity Nikolay Rostov does or says is good, intelligent, natural and moving; but everything Napoleon does and thinks is unnatural, unintelligent, inflated and of paltry significance.' It would be ridiculous to suppose that Chekhov resented Tolstoy's belittling of Napoleon—he did not care for wars or generals or cheap romanticism. What he resented was the violation of the laws of art: all Tolstoy's characters are drawn from the inside, they are alive and real, whereas Napoleon is shown from the outside and seems to have found his way accidentally from the poster to the artist's canvas.

Chekhov's sympathies and antagonisms are clear, but he does not touch up the people he likes and he finds human traits in those he dislikes or even hates. When critics used to say (as some still do) that his attitude to his heroes betrays coldness, they themselves betray their own coldness to genuine art.

Yes, Chekhov often said that the writer must remain cold while working. Quoting these words, Bunin adds: 'But, of course, it was a very special coldness. . . . For how many Russian writers have a moral sensibility and a responsiveness greater than Chekhov's?' What was this 'coldness' Chekhov talked about? As a youth of nineteen he wrote to his brother about *Uncle Tom's Cabin*: 'I had read it ages ago but I re-read it six months ago for scientific reasons, and afterwards I had the unpleasant sensation that mortals feel after eating too many sugar plums or raisins.' The reason why the youth felt nauseated was not, of course, that he supported slavery: no, but while agreeing with Harriet Beecher Stowe's ideas he could not bear counterfeit art. In 1892 he tried to explain to the young writer Lydia Avilova: 'There's just one thing. Here's my advice as a reader: when you portray unfortunate, dispossessed people and you want to move the reader's heart, try to be colder—this gives a sort of background to other men's sorrows against which they stand out in greater relief. As it is, your heroes weep and you sigh with them. Yes, be cold.' Lydia Avilova failed to understand the remark about 'coldness', and Chekhov patiently returned to the issue: 'I once said to you that when one writes sad stories one must be unmoved, and you did not understand me. One may weep and groan over one's own story, one may suffer with one's heroes, but I believe this should be done in such a way that the reader does not notice it.' I may add that these letters belong to the period when Chekhov was working on *Ward No. 6*. This story had and still has a tremendous emotional impact on the reader. Can anyone for an instant believe that the author did not share the sufferings of Dr Ragin and Ivan Dmitrich? Can anyone say that *Ward No. 6* is a work devoid of passion, of an idea? Lenin was twenty-two when the story appeared in print. Here is his impression: 'When I finished reading this story last night, a kind of terror seized me; I could not stay in my room, I got up and went out. I felt as if I, too, were shut up in Ward No. 6.'

—Ilya Ehrenburg, *Chekhov, Stendhal and Other Essays*, translated by Anna Bostock and Yvonne Kapp (London: Macgibbon & Kee, 1962): 40–41.

Maurice Valency on the World of *The Cherry Orchard*

[Maurice Valency is Professor Emeritus of Dramatic Literature, Columbia University, and Director of Academic Studies at the Julliard School. He is the author of works on Chekhov, Ibsen, Strindberg, Shaw, and medieval literature. He is also a playwright and librettist. In this passage, Valency discusses the world of *The Cherry Orchard* as a world decaying and transforming.]

The Cherry Orchard, like *The Three Sisters*, describes a world in transition. It depicts the terminal stages in the disintegration of a nest of gentlefolk, and the end of their way of life. From a descriptive viewpoint, it covers the situation quite thoroughly. It composes on a single canvas all the elements that bridge the gap between the old order and the new, and includes a gallery of unforgettable portraits, some of them familiar through the works of Turgenev, Goncharov, and Pisemsky, some of them original. It would hardly be possible in a play of this sort to avoid the inclusion of certain stereotypes of the social novel of the period. Ranyevskaya, for example, makes no effect of novelty. Pishchik, the perpetually astonished man; Gaev, with his imaginary game of billiards; the congenitally clumsy Epikhodov, Jean, the Frenchified valet; Dunyasha, the pretty soubrette—these were all vaudeville types; and both Firs, the faithful retainer, and Trofimov, the perpetual student, were by now conventional in Russian fiction. What was new in *The Cherry Orchard* was not the characters, nor the situation, but the way in which these were treated. It was precisely that blend of comedy and pathos with which, as it seemed to Chekhov, Stanislavsky was ruining his play, that gave *The Cherry Orchard* its originality and freshness.

The tendency toward portrait-painting which is a chief characteristic of Russian drama in the nineteenth century is nowhere so well exemplified as in *The Cherry Orchard*. None of the people represented is entirely simple. Chekhov evidently meant them all to seem at least a little ridiculous, but he treated them all with courtesy, and one suspects that he liked these characters very much, particularly Trofimov and Lopakhin, the theorist and the practical man.

Lopakhin is by way of becoming a millionaire, though he can hardly write his name. He is strong and shrewd, but he cannot summon up the courage to propose marriage to Varya, who is a member of the upper class, if only by adoption. Obviously, Varya is quite a handful. She is said to have the soul of a nun; and Lopakhin cannily prefers to torture her a little rather than to be tortured by her. In the scene by the chapel in the fields, when Lyubov congratulates her on her coming marriage with Lopakhin, Varya bursts into tears. He has not asked her yet. But instead of taking advantage of this golden opportunity to make her a definite proposal, Lopakhin pokes fun at her cruelly, playing a clownish Hamlet for her benefit:

> LOPAKHIN: Okhmelia, get you to a monastery!
> GAEV: Oh, look how my hands are shaking: it's a long time since I had a game of billiards.
> LOPAKHIN: Okhmelia, nymph, remember me in you prayers!
> LYUBOV ANDREYEVNA: Come, gentlemen. It's nearly supper time.

Lopakhin is not a kindly man, after all, and though Chekhov described him to Olga as a soft man, he is not soft. He has the brutality of the *muzhik*, and he plays sadistically with the woman who wishes to marry him, much as Chekhov once played with his women, though with less subtlety. From time to time, we catch a glimpse of the steel in Lopakhin, and we understand how it is he has become so rich so quickly. He is brisk with the servants, and pitiless with Gaev; and he prods Trofimov mercilessly, though it is clear he likes him. He worships Lyubov, and can refuse her nothing, though he has given her up for lost. It is clear that she is the secret love of his life, his ideal of womanhood, and perhaps the true reason why he will not compromise by marrying Varya.

Lopakhin is, above all, a workman. There is an unspoken sympathy between him and Trofimov, though they belong to different camps, and cannot communicate, and perhaps are fated to destroy one another.

—Maurice Valency, *The Breaking String: The Plays of Anton Chekhov* (New York: Oxford University Press, 1966): 271–273.

John Tulloch on *The Cherry Orchard* in a Political Scheme

[John Tulloch is the editor of *Conflict and Control in The Cinema: A Reader in Film and Society*, and the author of *Chekhov: A Study*. In this chapter, Tulloch discusses the world of *The Cherry Orchard* and its characters within a political scheme.]

The cherry orchard is confronted with the modern capitalist and the modern revolutionary. The question of choice, and with it the crisis of identity, while remaining individual is subsumed within broader social movements.

Each character typifies a social position in his response to the orchard. Trofimov sees in the trees dead souls; Lopakhin sees in them the opportunity for technology and growth; Madame Ranevskaya thinks only of style, elegance and the white figures of the past; Varya, a girl raised above her station by the kindly condescension of a status-conscious society, thinks only of saving that order through petty cheeseparing and recourse to religion, its official ideology. To say, however, that Chekhov poses the question of individual choice within the framework of social movements is not to interpret his play in the light of a straightforward class struggle. Chekhov is favouring neither an aristocratic, nor a bourgeois, nor a proletarian solution.

By choosing the decay of a landed estate (and the complete inability of the old landowners to come to terms with the problem of farming without serfs) for his theme, Chekhov was not only selecting a problem about which he had written more than once, and of which he had a close personal experience, but also a typical contradiction of a society which tried to modernise yet, in terms of social stratification, stay the same. The *situation* in *The Cherry Orchard* is the moment when the autonomous world of tradition has been breached by the serf reforms and the will to modernise; when in Firs' words, 'everything is muddled', and the action must be rational and decisive, yet within mores and institutions which remain ascriptive. The reactions of each landowner to the problem of debt differ at the personal level—Ranevskaya escapes to Paris, Gayev into dreams of liberal gentry and superfluous men, Simeonov-Pishchik into money-grubbing and a hand-to-mouth existence from day to day while he waits for something to turn up. But *socially* their reactions are qualitatively the same. They are simply incapable of adapting to the demands of a new rationality; Pishchik is as incapable of entrepreneurial activity when profitable minerals are discovered on his land, as Madame Ranevskaya is of profiting from the spread of new urban wealth to the country. Essentially they are people preoccupied with the old style of life, servants in livery, large tips to the waiters, casual philanthropy and amateur medical treatment for the poor—people who act from day to day, move from place to place, but really stay the same. ⟨. . .⟩

In their isolation the landowners are marginal and anomic figures. Ranevskaya, the aristocratic woman who married beneath her station, travels from place to place seeking purpose in locations and in a lover who cheats her. Faced with the sale of the orchard she retreats into her past when everything was elegant and certain. Gayev also retreats into the past, given an extra and pompous dignity by his references to learning and social service. But his relationship to reason and the Enlightenment is empty; it goes no further than justifying the continued existence of the unproductive orchard on the grounds that it was mentioned in the Encyclopaedia. For all his escape into a pathetic flow of words, his refrain, 'I'll be silent, I'll be silent', is that of a man lost. Anya is aroused by the revolutionary ideals of Trofimov, but the vision of a new life of this naive girl is strangely mixed with the intention of planting another orchard and living happily ever after with her mother as they read to each other in the long evenings. Varya is divided between a desperate attempt to save the old order, to which she would somehow or other attach Lopakhin, and a desire to escape into the nun-like existence of Ol'ga in *Big Volodya and Little Volodya*. Increasing mobility within this crumbling, self-conscious structure simply intensifies social marginality which, in the absence of a confident and coherent symbolic system becomes spiritual anomie as each individual faces alone the meaninglessness of his existence.

But there is little tragedy. Spiritual isolation is signified by a comic failure of communication when characters are *collectively* faced with the reality of change. So when Lopakhin first suggests the need to cut down the cherry orchard and let the land for summer villas, the reaction among the landowners is a comic and trivial dialogue of escape. Firs speaks of an old recipe for drying cherries; Ranevskaya asks for the recipe, but it is lost. Pishchik then asks whether they ate frogs in Paris, and Ranevskaya says she ate crocodiles, which Pishchik greets with great wonder. Lopakhin tries again with his plan. Gayev replies 'what idiocy!' and after a brief exchange between Varya and Ranevskaya which reveals both the former's workaday ritual and the latter's asylum in Paris, Gayev launches into his famous oration to the old and venerable bookcase which has been the source of his family's devotion to the people for so long. Silenced by Lopakhin's irony, he retreats into his billiard talk, and almost immediately the remaining landowner, Pishchik, reveals his extraordinary unconcern for the realities of life (and medical science!) by swallowing all of Ranevskaya's pills. Each individual responds quite typically to Lopakhin's suggestion; and each response reveals inner isolation. Yet the interaction, revealed as a collective style of life, is comic and absurd. The private worlds of Ranevskaya, Gayev, Varya and Pishchik, sad and lyrical though they may be, are a focus of irrationality, and thus, situationally, of the absurd.

—John Tulloch, *Chekhov: A Structuralist Study* (New York: Harper and Row, 1980): 185–188.

DONALD RAYFIELD ON THE IDEAS BEHIND *THE CHERRY ORCHARD*

[Donald Rayfield is a professor of Russian literature at Queen Mary and Westfield College, University of London. His books include *Chekhov: The Evolution of His Art*, and *The Cherry Orchard: Catastrophe and Comedy*. In this passage, Rayfield gives some of Chekhov's original ideas about *The Cherry Orchard* and a broad overview.]

By September ⟨1903⟩, despite his painfully slow pace, Anton was sure of his plan for *The Cherry Orchard*. He warned Stanislvasky's wife: 'At places it is even a farce; I fear I shall get it in the neck from Nemirovich-Danchenko.' Stanislavsky feared worse, telling his sister Zinaida on 7 September: 'I imagine it will be something impossible on the weirdness and vulgarity of life. I only fear that instead of a farce again we shall have a great big tragedy. Even now he thinks *Three Sisters* a very merry little piece.'

Like *The Seagull*, *The Cherry Orchard* is subtitled 'comedy', even though it focuses on the destruction of a family and their illusions. The new play is crowded with reminiscence of earlier work and of personal traumas. The cherry trees that blossom in Act I recall those of his boyhood in Taganrog; the cherry trees axed in Act 4 recall the trees of Melikhovo, bought ten years earlier and now felled by Konshin. ⟨. . .⟩

An elegy for a lost world, estate and class, *The Cherry Orchard* nevertheless displays Anton's farcical invention at its richest. As in all Chekhovian comedy, however, the ending is grim, for the old retain power while the young are scattered to the winds. One factor alone is missing from the play: passion. Only the mistress of the house, Ranevskaia, who comes to Russia from her love in France and then leaves again, is a sexual being. Nobody else expresses ardour, any more than Charlotta's rifle or Epikhodov's revolver ever fire. The doctor, increasingly inert in Chekhov's plays, fails to call. Death, in an ending which heralds Samuel Beckett, is banal: a senile servant is forgotten in a locked house. Black humour, menace, wistfulness, the characters' doll-like quadrilles, the dominance of landscape over inhabitants; all these qualities make *The Cherry Orchard* the progenitor of modern drama from Artaud to Pinter. The engineer Garin-Mikhailovsky saw the same incongruity between Anton's creative imagination and his doom as we see in the owners of *The Cherry Orchard*. He noted: 'Chekhov could hardly walk, noises came from his chest. but he seemed not to notice. He was interested in anything but illness: . . . Why are such precious contents locked up in such a frail vessel?' ⟨. . .⟩

He was finishing *The Cherry Orchard* with pleasure—for once ending a play not with a gun, but an axe—but he was tormented by his cough and pains in his muscles. Altshuller forbade him to wash, applied Spanish fly and beseeched him not to go to Moscow. Anton would ignore this advice.

> —Donald Rayfield, *Anton Chekhov: A Life* (New York: Henry Holt and Company 1997): 579–581.

Works by Anton Chekhov

Chekhov only wrote seven full-length plays, and of the seven only the four appearing in this study guide are considered canonical. The other three are not considered on a par with these four and his eleven one-act plays are not as widely read and are rarely performed.

In addition to the plays listed here, however, Checkhov wrote almost 500 short stories. Many of these stories are considered more important and are more widely read than his lesser plays, especially since his short stories were often studies for his larger plays.

These are listed in the order they were written and published.

Platonov. 1881.

On the Highway. 1885.

On the Harmful Effects of Tobacco. 1886.

Swan Song. 1887.

The Bear. 1888.

Ivanov. 1889.

The Proposal. 1889.

Tatiana Repina. 1889.

The Tragedian. in Spite of Himself 1889.

The Wood Demon. 1889.

The Night Before the Trial. 1890s (unfinished).

The Wedding. 1890.

The Anniversary. 1891.

The Celebration. 1891.

Uncle Vanya. Published in 1897, premiered in 1899.

The Three Sisters. Published in 1901, premiered in 1901.

The Seagull. Published in 1903, premiered in 1896.

The Cherry Orchard. Published in 1904, premiered in 1904.

Works about Anton Chekhov

Avilov, Lydia. *Chekhov in My Life: A Love Story.* Translated with and introduction by David Magarshak. London: J. Lehman, 1950.

Barricelli, Jean-Pierre, ed. *Checkhov's Great Plays: A Critical Anthology.* New York: New York University Press, 1981.

Bentley, Eric. *In Search of Theater.* New York: Alfred A. Knopf, 1953.

Bitsilli, Peter. *Checkhov's Art: A Stylistic Analysis.* trans. Toby Clyman and Edwina Jannie Cruise. Ann Arbor, MI: Ardis Publishers, 1983.

Bristow, Eugene K., ed. *Anton Chekhov's Plays.* New York: W. W. Norton & Company, 1977.

Bruford, W. H. *Chekhov and His Russia: A Sociological Study.* New York: Oxford University Press, 1948.

Charques, Richard. *The Twilight of Imperial Russia.* New York: Oxford University Press, 1950.

Eekman, T. ed., *Anton Cechov, 1860–1960: Some Essays.* Leiden: E. J. Brill, 1960.

Ehrenburg, Ilya. *Chekhov, Stendhal and Other Essays,* trans. by Anna Bostock and Yvonne Kapp. London: Macgibbon & Kee, 1962.

Fergusson, Francis. *The Idea of Theater.* Princeton, NJ: Princeton University Press, 1949.

Gerhardi, William. *Anton Chekhov: A Critical Study.* London: Macdonald & Co., 1949.

Gilman, Richard. *Chekhov's Plays: An Opening into Eternity.* New Haven: Yale University Press, 1995.

Gorky, Maxim. *Reminiscences of Tolstoy, Chekhov and Andreev,* trans. by Katherine Mansfield, S. S. Koteliansky, and Leonard Woolf. London: The Hogarth Press, 1948.

Hingley, Ronald. *Russian Writers and Society 1825–1904.* New York: McGraw-Hill Book Company, 1967.

———. *Chekhov: A Biographical and Critical Study.* London: George Allen & Unwin, 1966.

Jackson, Robert Louis, ed. *Reading Chekhov's Text*. Evanston, IL: Northwestern University Press. 1993

———. *Chekhov: A Collection of Critical Essays*. Englewood Cliffs, NJ: Prentice-Hall, 1967.

Karlinsky, Simon, ed. *Anton Chekhov's Life and Thought: Selected Letters and Commentary*. Translated by Henry Heim and Simon Karlinsky. Berkeley: University of California Press, 1973.

Kirk, Irina. *Anton Chekhov*. Boston: Twayne Publishers, 1981.

Lafitte, Sophie. *Tchekhov 1860–1904*. Paris: Librarie Hatchette, 1971.

Magarshack, David. *Chekhov the Dramatist*. New York: Hill and Wang, 1960.

———. *Chekhov: A Life*. New York: Grove Press, 1955.

———. *The Real Chekhov: An Introduction to Chekhov's Last Plays*. London: George Allen & Unwin, 1972.

Melchinger, Siegfried. *Anton Chekhov*. New York: Frederick Ungar Publishing, 1972.

Nemirovitch-Dantchenko, Vladimir. *My Life in the Russian Theatre*. Translated by John Cournos. New York: Theater Arts Books, 1968.

Peace, Richard. *Chekhov: A Study of the Four Major Plays*. New Haven: Yale University Press, 1983.

Rayfield, Donald. *Anton Chekhov: A Life*. New York: Henry Holt and Company, 1997.

———. *Chekhov: The Evolution of His Art*. New York: Barnes and Noble, 1975.

Simmons, Ernest J. *Chekhov: A Biography*. Boston: Little, Brown and Company, 1962.

Smith, Virginia Llewellyn. *Anton Chekhov and the Lady with the Dog*. London: Oxford University Press, 1973.

Stanislavsky, Konstantin. *Stanislavsky on the Art of the Stage*. Translated by David Magarshack. London, 1950.

Styan, J. L. *Chekhov in Performance: A Commentary on the Major Plays*. Cambridge: Cambridge University Press, 1971.

Toumanova, Princess Nina Andronikova. *Anton Checkhov: The Voice of Twilight Russia.* New York: Columbia University Press, 1937.

Tulloch, John. *Chekhov: A Structuralist Study.* New York: Harper and Row Publishers, 1980.

Valency, Maurice. *The Breaking String: The Plays of Anton Chekhov.* New York: Oxford University Press, 1966.

Winner, Thomas. *Chekhov and His Prose.* New York: Holt, Rinehart and Winston, 1966.

Yermilov, Vladimir. *Anton Pavlovich Chekhov 1860–1904.* Moscow: Foreign Languages Publishing House, 1959.

Index of Themes and Ideas

CHEKHOV, ANTON: biography of, 11–13; cautious optimism of, 68–70; melodrama and farce and, 44–46; Moscow Art Theater and, 26–27, 42–43, 69; religion and, 66–68; shadings of character in works of, 90–92; Shakespeare and, 9–10, 15–17, 24, 94; Stanislavsky and, 42–43, 69, 93, 97–98; tragic humor of, 86–88

CHERRY ORCHARD, THE, 13, 79–98; characters in, 84–85; critical views on, 9, 10, 44, 66, 86–98; decaying and transforming world of, 93–94; Dunyasha in, 80, 81, 85, 93; Firs in, 81, 83, 85, 93, 95, 96–97; Leonid Andreevich Gaev in, 80, 81, 83, 84, 89, 93, 94, 95, 96, 97; Grisha in, 80, 82; ideas behind, 97–98; Sharlotta Ivanovna in, 80, 81, 85, 98; Yermolay Alexeevich Lopakhin in, 5, 10, 79, 80, 81, 82, 83, 84, 89, 90, 93–94, 96, 97; melodrama and farce and, 44; plot summary of, 79–83; political scheme and, 95–97; Anya Ranevskaya in, 79, 80, 83, 84, 89, 90, 96; Lyubov Andreevna Ranevskaya in, 10, 79, 80, 81, 83, 84, 88, 89, 90, 94, 95, 96, 97, 98; Varya Ranevskaya in, 79, 80, 81, 83, 84, 88, 89, 94, 95, 96, 97; religion and, 66; Shakespeare and, 9, 10; Boris Borisovich Simeonov-Pishchik in, 85, 93, 95–96, 97; suffering of change in, 88–90; tragic humor in, 88; Pyotr Sergeevich Trofimov in, 82, 83, 84–85, 88, 90, 93, 94, 95, 96; Yasha in, 81, 83, 85; Semyon Panteleevich Yepikhodor in, 81, 85

SEAGULL, THE, 12–13, 14–34, 43; Polina Andreevna in, 20, 27, 32; Irina Nikolaevna Arkadina in, 14, 15–16, 17, 19, 21, 26, 27, 28, 29–31; art as subject in, 23–25, 32–34; cautious optimism in, 68; characters in, 19–20; critical views on, 9, 21–34, 46–47, 68, 98; Yevgeny Sergeevich Dorn in, 17, 18, 20, 25, 26, 27, 28, 31, 32; first production of, 21–23; Masha in, 14, 15, 16, 17, 20, 21, 26, 27, 28, 29, 30, 32, 46, 47; Maupassant's travel sketch, Sur l'eau in, 28–30; Semyon Semyonovich Medvedenko in, 14, 15, 16, 17, 20, 21, 26, 27; Moscow Art Theater and, 26–27; plot summary of, 14–18; Shakespeare and, 9, 16–17, 24; Ilya Afansevich Shamraev in, 16, 20, 21, 26, 27, 29, 30–32; Pytor Nikloaevich Sorin in, 14, 15, 16, 17, 19, 21; Konstantin Gavrilovich Treplyov in, 9, 15, 16–17, 18, 19, 21, 22, 24–25, 26, 27, 29, 30, 31, 32–34, 46–47; Boris Alekseevich Trigorin in, 9, 15–16, 17, 18, 20, 21, 25, 26, 27, 28, 29, 30, 31, 32, 34, 68; Nina Mikhaylovna Zarechnaya in, 9, 15–16, 17, 18, 19, 22–23, 25, 26–27, 29, 31, 32–34, 68

THREE SISTERS, THE, 58–78; Anfisa in, 62, 65; Bobik in, 76; cautious optimism in, 68–69, 70; characters in, 63–65; Ivan Romanovich Chebutykin in, 59, 60, 64, 73–74, 75, 77; comedy and tragedy in, 77–78; critical views on, 9–10, 44, 47, 55, 56, 66–68, 87–88, 93; Alexey Petrovich Fedotik in, 64; Ferapont in, 64–65; grouping of characters in, 75–76; Natalya (Natasha) Ivanovna in, 58, 60, 61, 62, 72–73, 74, 76; Fyodor Ilich Kulygin in, 59, 63–64, 76; melodrama and farce and, 44; Moscow in, 71–72; plot summary of, 58–62; Protopopov in, 62, 74, 76; Irina Prozorov in, 9–10, 58, 60, 61, 62, 63, 68, 71, 72, 73–74, 75, 76; Masha Prozorov in, 9–10, 58, 59, 63, 71, 72, 73, 75, 76; Olga Prozorov in, 9–10, 47, 55, 58, 60, 61, 62, 63, 71, 72, 75, 76, 87–88; religion and, 66; Vladimir Karlovich Rode in, 64; Andrey Sergeevich in, 9–10, 58, 60, 61, 62, 63, 71, 72–73, 75–76, 77; Shakespeare and, 9–10; Captain Vasily Vasilevich Solyony in, 59, 61–62, 64, 75, 76, 77, 88; tragic humor in, 87–88; Baron Nikolay Lvovich Tuzenbakh in, 5, 59, 60, 61, 62, 64, 68–69, 74, 76, 77, 88; Alexandr Ignatevich Vershinin in, 48, 56, 59–60, 62, 64, 70, 71–72, 73, 76, 77–78, 88

UNCLE VANYA, 13, 35–57; Sofya (Sonya) Alexandrovna in, 35, 36, 38–39, 40, 49, 52–54; Yelena Andreevna in, 36, 37, 38, 40, 45, 46, 49, 50, 51–54; Mikhail Lvovich Astrov in, 35, 36–37, 38, 41, 47–48, 49–50, 51, 54, 56; beauty in, 49–51; cautious optimism in, 68; characters in, 40–41; critical views on, 9, 42–57; hope for a better life in, 54–57; hopelessness in, 46–48; melodrama and farce in, 45; plot summary of, 35–39; Alexandr Vladimirovich Serebryakov in, 35, 36, 37–38, 40, 46, 54; Shakespeare and, 9; Ilya Ilich Telegin in, 36, 38, 39, 41, 54; Ivan Petrovich (Vanya) Voynitsky in, 35–36, 37–38, 39, 40–41, 45, 46, 48, 49, 50–51, 53, 54, 68; Yelena's attitude toward work in, 51–54